Blend-It Books

Houghton Mifflin Harcourt™

Printed in the U.S.A.

ISBN 978-0-544-58641-3

6 7 8 9 10 0982 24 23 22 21 20 19 18 17 16
4500588589 B C D E F G

What is the purpose of the Blend-It Books?

The **Blend-It Books** provide engaging, highly decodable texts (75% or more decodable words) for independent blending and reading practice, to promote decoding automaticity and fluency. For each sound-spelling taught in Grade 1 of the Houghton Mifflin Harcourt *Journeys* program, two four-page books feature the skill within connected text. For sounds with multiple spellings, two sound-spellings are sometimes paired in the same books for comparison. For example, there are two books for the short *o* sound. For the long *o* sound, there are two books for the *o* and *o_e* spellings, and two more books for the *ow* and *oa* spellings taught at this grade.

In addition, the **Blend-It Books** provide practice for key structural analysis skills. For example, for the *-ed* inflection there are two books for *each* pronunciation: /ĕd/, /d/, and /t/. Later in the year, two more books feature *-ed*, this time using words with spelling changes (dropped final *e*, doubled final consonant) before the inflection.

The text for each book also includes a smaller number (25% or fewer) of high-frequency words taught previously in *Journeys*. Those words were drawn from research studies on the most commonly used words in English, and words were chosen only when they received high scores on multiple lists.

For reference, the back of each book lists all the decodable words, decoding skills, and high-frequency words featured in that selection. A summary list inside the back cover shows all the decoding skills and high-frequency words taught to date in *Journeys*.

How are the Blend-It Books organized?

The **Blend-It Books** are numbered sequentially and reflect the order of the decoding skills taught in each unit of *Journeys*. The chart on the following pages lists all the books for Grade 1.

Volume 1: Books 1–112 for the skills in Units 1–3
Volume 2: Books 113–200 for the skills in Units 4–6

When do I use the Blend-It Books?

- Users of *Journeys* will find references to corresponding **Blend-It Books** in the phonics lessons in the Teacher's Editions.
- The books are also an excellent resource any time a child needs extra practice reading words with a specific sound/spelling.

How can I use Blend-It Books to meet specific needs?

- Help children differentiate between two or more similar sound/spellings by reading and comparing books that feature them.
- Have English learners focus on sounds and spellings they find difficult in English by reading books chorally with an adult.
- Informally assess children's understanding of a new skill by having them read a book aloud to you.

What are the options for setting up the Blend-It Books?

- The books are available as blackline masters for copying, or in digital files that can be read onscreen or downloaded.
- Provide children with the books only as they need them, or set up the numbered books for children to access on their own all year.
- Make copies for children to read and color in class or take home, or prepare a laminated set for use at school.
- Set up a chart for children to track their own progress as they read.

This chart lists all the Grade 1 **Blend-It Books** (both volumes) and identifies books that correspond to the *Journeys* Sound/Spelling Cards.

Book	Skill	Sound/Spelling Cards
Book 1	*m, s, t, c,* short *a*	Mouse, Seal, Tiger, Cat, Apple
Book 2	*m, s, t, c,* short *a*	Mouse, Seal, Tiger, Cat, Apple
Book 3	consonant *n*	Noodles
Book 4	consonant *n*	Noodles
Book 5	consonant *d*	Duck
Book 6	consonant *d*	Duck
Book 7	consonant *p*	Pig
Book 8	consonant *p*	Pig
Book 9	consonant *f*	Fish
Book 10	consonant *f*	Fish
Book 11	short *i*	Igloo
Book 12	short *i*	Igloo
Book 13	consonant *r*	Rooster
Book 14	consonant *r*	Rooster
Book 15	consonant *h*	Horse
Book 16	consonant *h*	Horse
Book 17	/z/ spelled *s*	Zebra
Book 18	/z/ spelled *s*	Zebra
Book 19	consonant *b*	Bear
Book 20	consonant *b*	Bear
Book 21	consonant *g*	Goose
Book 22	consonant *g*	Goose
Book 23	short *o*	Ostrich
Book 24	short *o*	Ostrich
Book 25	consonant *l*	Lion
Book 26	consonant *l*	Lion
Book 27	consonant *x*	Fox
Book 28	consonant *x*	Fox
Book 29	inflection *-s*	

Book	Skill	Sound/Spelling Cards
Book 30	inflection *-s*	
Book 31	short *e*	Elephant
Book 32	short *e*	Elephant
Book 33	consonant *y*	Yo-yo
Book 34	consonant *y*	Yo-yo
Book 35	consonant *w*	Worm
Book 36	consonant *w*	Worm
Book 37	consonant *k*	Kangaroo
Book 38	consonant *k*	Kangaroo
Book 39	consonant *v*	Volcano
Book 40	consonant *v*	Volcano
Book 41	consonant *j*	Jump
Book 42	consonant *j*	Jump
Book 43	short *u*	Umbrella
Book 44	short *u*	Umbrella
Book 45	/kw/ spelled *qu*	Queen
Book 46	/kw/ spelled *qu*	Queen
Book 47	consonant *z*	Zebra
Book 48	consonant *z*	Zebra
Book 49	final consonants *ll*	Lion
Book 50	final consonants *ll*	Lion
Book 51	final consonants *ss*	Seal
Book 52	final consonants *ss*	Seal
Book 53	consonants *ck*	Kangaroo
Book 54	consonants *ck*	Kangaroo
Book 55	final consonants *ff*	Fish
Book 56	final consonants *ff*	Fish
Book 57	final consonants *zz*	Zebra
Book 58	final consonants *zz*	Zebra
Book 59	blends with *r*	
Book 60	blends with *r*	

Book	Skill	Sound/Spelling Cards
Book 61	blends with *l*	
Book 62	blends with *l*	
Book 63	blends with *s*	
Book 64	blends with *s*	
Book 65	final blend *mp*	
Book 66	final blend *mp*	
Book 67	final blend *nt*	
Book 68	final blend *nt*	
Book 69	final blend *nd*	
Book 70	final blend *nd*	
Book 71	final blend *st*	
Book 72	final blend *st*	
Book 73	digraph *th*	Thumb
Book 74	digraph *th*	Thumb
Book 75	ending *-s*	
Book 76	ending *-s*	
Book 77	ending *-es*	
Book 78	ending *-es*	
Book 79	ending *-ed*/ĕd/	
Book 80	ending *-ed*/ĕd/	
Book 81	ending *-ed* /d/	Duck
Book 82	ending *-ed* /d/	Duck
Book 83	ending *-ed* /t/	Tiger
Book 84	ending *-ed* /t/	Tiger
Book 85	ending *-ing*	
Book 86	ending *-ing*	
Book 87	digraphs *ch, tch*	Chick
Book 88	digraphs *ch, tch*	Chick
Book 89	possessives with *'s*	
Book 90	possessives with *'s*	
Book 91	digraph *sh*	Sheep

Book	Skill	Sound/Spelling Cards
Book 92	digraph *sh*	Sheep
Book 93	digraph *wh*	Whale
Book 94	digraph *wh*	Whale
Book 95	digraph *ph*	Fish
Book 96	digraph *ph*	Fish
Book 97	contractions *'s, n't*	
Book 98	contractions *'s, n't*	
Book 99	long *a* (CVC*e*)	Acorn
Book 100	long *a* (CVC*e*)	Acorn
Book 101	soft *c* /s/	Seal
Book 102	soft *c* /s/	Seal
Book 103	/j/ spelled *g, dge*	Jump
Book 104	/j/ spelled *g, dge*	Jump
Book 105	long *i* (CVC*e*)	Ice Cream
Book 106	long *i* (CVC*e*)	Ice Cream
Book 107	digraphs *kn, gn*	Noodles
Book 108	digraphs *kn, gn*	Noodles
Book 109	digraph *wr*	Rooster
Book 110	digraph *wr*	Rooster
Book 111	digraph *mb*	Mouse
Book 112	digraph *mb*	Mouse
Book 113	long *o* (CV, CVC*e*)	Ocean
Book 114	long *o* (CV, CVC*e*)	Ocean
Book 115	long *u* (CVC*e*)	Uniform
Book 116	long *u* (CVC*e*)	Uniform
Book 117	long *e* (*e, ee*)	Eagle
Book 118	long *e* (*e, ee*)	Eagle
Book 119	long *e* (CVC*e, ea*)	Eagle
Book 120	long *e* (CVC*e, ea*)	Eagle

Book	Skill	Sound/Spelling Cards
Book 121	final consonants *ng*	Ring
Book 122	final consonants *ng*	Ring
Book 123	final consonants *nk*	
Book 124	final consonants *nk*	
Book 125	long *a* (*ai, ay*)	Acorn
Book 126	long *a* (*ai, ay*)	Acorn
Book 127	contractions *'ll, 'd*	
Book 128	contractions *'ll, 'd*	
Book 129	long *o* (*ow, oa*)	Ocean
Book 130	long *o* (*ow, oa*)	Ocean
Book 131	contractions *'ve, 're*	
Book 132	contractions *'ve, 're*	
Book 133	compound words	
Book 134	compound words	
Book 135	short *e* (*ea*)	Elephant
Book 136	short *e* (*ea*)	Elephant
Book 137	*r*-controlled *ar*	Artist
Book 138	*r*-controlled *ar*	Artist
Book 139	*r*-controlled *or, ore*	Orange
Book 140	*r*-controlled *or, ore*	Orange
Book 141	*r*-controlled *er, ir*	Bird
Book 142	*r*-controlled *er, ir*	Bird
Book 143	*r*-controlled *ur*	Bird
Book 144	*r*-controlled *ur*	Bird
Book 145	/o͝o/ spelled *oo*	Cook
Book 146	/o͝o/ spelled *oo*	Cook
Book 147	closed syllables (CVC)	
Book 148	closed syllables (CVC)	

Book	Skill	Sound/Spelling Cards
Book 149	/ōō/ spelled *ou, ew*	Moon
Book 150	/ōō/ spelled *ou, ew*	Moon
Book 151	/ōō/ spelled *oo*	Moon
Book 152	/ōō/ spelled oo	Moon
Book 153	/ōō/ spelled *u, ue*	Moon
Book 154	/ōō/ spelled *u, ue*	Moon
Book 155	/ōō/ spelled *u_e* (CVC*e*)	Moon
Book 156	/ōō/ spelled *u_e* (CVCe)	Moon
Book 157	/ou/ spelled *ou, ow*	Owl
Book 158	/ou/ spelled *ou, ow*	Owl
Book 159	/oi/ spelled *oy, oi*	Boy
Book 160	/oi/ spelled *oy, oi*	Boy
Book 161	/aw/ spelled *aw, au*	Saw
Book 162	/aw/ spelled *aw, au*	Saw
Book 163	ending *-ing*: drop *e*; double consonant	
Book 164	ending *-ing*: drop *e*; double consonant	
Book 165	ending *-ed*: drop *e*; double consonant	
Book 166	ending *-ed*: drop *e*; double consonant	
Book 167	long *e* spelled *y, ie*	Eagle
Book 168	long *e* spelled *y, ie*	Eagle
Book 169	endings *-es, -ed*: change *y* to *i*	
Book 170	endings *-es, -ed*: change *y* to *i*	
Book 171	ending *-er*	
Book 172	ending *-er*	

Book	Skill	Sound/Spelling Cards
Book 173	ending *-est*	
Book 174	ending *-est*	
Book 175	ending *-er*: drop *e*; double consonant	
Book 176	ending *-er*: drop *e*; double consonant	
Book 177	ending *-est*: drop *e*; double consonant	
Book 178	ending *-est*: drop *e*; double consonant	
Book 179	endings *-er*, *-est*: change *y* to *i*	
Book 180	endings *-er*, *-est*: change *y* to *i*	
Book 181	syllable *_le*	Table
Book 182	syllable *_le*	Table
Book 183	long *i* spelled *ie, igh*	Ice Cream
Book 184	long *i* spelled *ie, igh*	Ice Cream
Book 185	long *i* spelled *y*	Ice Cream
Book 186	long *i* spelled *y*	Ice Cream
Book 187	long *i* spelled *y*: change to *i*, add *-es*, *-ed*	
Book 188	long *i* spelled *y*: change to *i*, add *-es*, *-ed*	
Book 189	suffix *-ful*	
Book 190	suffix *-ful*	
Book 191	suffix *-ly*	
Book 192	suffix *-ly*	
Book 193	suffix *-y*	
Book 194	suffix *-y*	
Book 195	open syllables (CV)	
Book 196	open syllables (CV)	
Book 197	prefix *un-*	
Book 198	prefix *un-*	
Book 199	prefix *re-*	
Book 200	prefix *re-*	

Sam Sat, Cat Sat

DECODABLE WORDS

Target Skill: **consonants *m*, *s*, *t*, *c*, short *a***

cat Sam sat

HIGH-FREQUENCY WORDS

go see

Houghton Mifflin Harcourt

m, *s*, *t*, *c*, short *a*

BOOK 1

Sam Sat, Cat Sat

High-Frequency Words Taught to Date

Grade 1

a	go	is	see	to
are	I	like	the	we

Decoding skills taught to date: consonants: *m*, *s*, *t*, *c*, short *a*

Sam sat.

Sam Sat, Cat Sat

Sam sat. Cat sat.

See Cat go!

Cat sat.

Cat! Cat! Cat!

DECODABLE WORDS

Target Skill: ***consonants m, s, t, c, short a***

Cam	Mac	sat
Cat	mat	Tam

HIGH-FREQUENCY WORDS

a	I	see

Houghton Mifflin Harcourt

m, s, t, c, short a

BOOK 2

Cat! Cat! Cat!

High-Frequency Words Taught to Date

Grade 1

a go is see to
are I like the we

Decoding skills taught to date: consonants: *m, s, t, c,* short *a*

Cat sat.

Cat! Cat! Cat!

I see a mat.

Cam sat. Tam sat. Mac sat.

Cat! Cat! Cat!

We Can

DECODABLE WORDS

Target Skill: **consonant *n***

can Nan Nat

Previously Taught Skills

(Words listed under **Target Skill** also include previously taught skills.)

SKILLS APPLIED IN WORDS IN STORY: consonants: *m, s, t, c,* short *a*; consonant *n*

HIGH-FREQUENCY WORDS

and we

Houghton Mifflin Harcourt

We Can

High-Frequency Words Taught to Date

Grade 1

a	go	like	to
and	help	play	we
are	I	see	with
be	is	the	you

Decoding skills taught to date: consonants: *m, s, t, c;* short *a*; consonant *n*

Nat and Nan can!

We Can

Nat can.

Nan can.

Nat can.

Nat

DECODABLE WORDS

Target Skill: **consonant *n***

Nan can Nat

Previously Taught Skills

SKILLS APPLIED IN WORDS IN STORY: consonants *t, c*; short *a*; consonant *n*

HIGH-FREQUENCY WORDS

and play

Houghton Mifflin Harcourt

consonant *n*

BOOK 4

Nat

High-Frequency Words Taught to Date

Grade 1

a	go	like	to
and	help	play	we
are	I	see	with
be	is	the	you

Decoding skills taught to date: consonants *m*, *s*, *t*, *c*; short *a*; consonant *n*

Nan and Nat can play!

Nat

Nan can.

Nan can.

Nat can!

Dan Can

DECODABLE WORDS

Target Skill: **consonant *d***

Dan Dad sad stand

Previously Taught Skills

at can sat

SKILLS APPLIED IN WORDS IN STORY: consonants: *s*, *t*, *c*; short *a*; consonant *n*; consonant *d*

HIGH-FREQUENCY WORDS

go is the

Houghton Mifflin Harcourt.

consonant *d*

BOOK 5

Dan Can

High-Frequency Words Taught to Date

Grade 1

a	go	like	to
and	help	play	we
are	I	see	with
be	is	the	you

Decoding skills taught to date: consonants: *m, s, t, c*; short *a*; consonant *n*; consonant *d*

Dan can! Dan can!

Dan Can

Dan sat. Dad sat.

Is Dan sad?

Dan is at the stand.

Go, Dan!

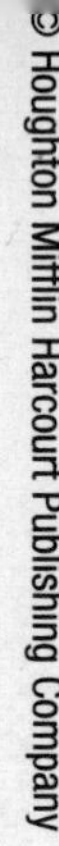

High-Frequency Words Taught to Date

Grade 1

a	cold	for	help	make	out	starts	watch
after	come	four	her	many	over	take	water
all	do	friend	here	me	own	the	we
and	does	full	hold	my	pictures	their	what
animal	down	funny	how	never	play	they	where
are	draw	give	I	new	pull	those	who
away	eat	go	into	no	put	three	why
be	every	goes	is	now	read	to	with
been	eyes	good	know	of	said	today	would
bird	fall	green	like	off	see	too	write
blue	far	grow	little	one	she	two	yellow
both	find	have	live	open	sing	very	you
brown	five	he	long	or	small	walk	
call	fly	hear	look	our	some	was	

Decoding skills taught to date: consonants *m, s, c, t*; short *a*; consonant *n*; consonant *d*; consonant *p*; consonant *f*; short *i*; consonant *r*; consonant *h*; /z/ spelled *s*; consonant *b*; consonant *g*; short *o*; consonant *l*; consonant *x*; inflection *-s;* short *e*; consonant *y*; consonant *w*; consonant *k*; consonant *v*; consonant *j*; short *u*; /kw/ spelled *qu*; consonant *z*; final consonants *ll*; double final consonants *ss*; consonants *ck*; final consonants *ff*; final consonants *zz*; blends with *r*; blends with *l*; blends with *s*; final blend *mp*; final blend *nt*; final blend *nd;* final blend *st*; digraph *th*; ending *-s*; ending *-es*; ending *-ed* /ed/; ending *-ed* /d/; ending *-ed* /t/; ending *-ing*; digraphs *ch, tch*; possessives with *'s*; digraph *sh*; digraph *wh*; digraph *ph*; contractions *'s, n't*; long *a* (CVC*e*); soft *c* /s/; /j/ spelled *g, dge*; long *i* (CVC*e*); digraphs *kn, gn*; digraph *wr*; digraph *mb*

Crumb Cake

DECODABLE WORDS

Target Skill: ***digraph mb***

crumb	crumbs	thumbs

Previously Taught Skills

add	cake	help	milk	steps
and	checks	in	mix	stuff
at	dump	is	Mom	then
bake	eggs	last	on	top
baked	from	lets	pan	with
bakes	get	make	shelf	yum

SKILLS APPLIED IN WORDS IN STORY: consonants *m, s, c, t*; short *a*; consonant *n*; consonant *d*; consonant *p*; consonant *f*; short *i*; consonant *r*; consonant *h*; /z/ spelled *s*; consonant *b*; consonant *g* (hard); short *o*; consonant *l*; consonant *x*; inflection *-s;* short *e*; consonant *y*; consonant *w*; consonant *k*; short *u*; consonants *-ck*; final consonants *ff*; blends with *r*; blends with *l*; blends with *s*; final blend *mp*; final blend *nd;* digraph *th*; ending -*s*; ending *-ed* /t/; digraph *ch*; long *a* (CVCe); long *i* (CVCe); digraph *mb*

HIGH-FREQUENCY WORDS

goes	of	put	to
me	our	the	we

Houghton Mifflin Harcourt

digraph *mb*

BOOK 112

Crumb Cake

I bump my thumb.
My thumb is numb.

Mom can help.
Mom fixes my thumb.

My thumb is fine. I am glad.
Lamb and I get back on
the limb.
Fun, fun, fun!

Lamb and I

I like to go up, up, up. I take
Lamb with me.
Lamb and I sit on a big limb.
Fun!

High-Frequency Words Taught to Date

Grade 1

a
after
all
and
animal
are
away
be
been
bird
blue
both
brown
call
cold
come
do
does
down
draw
eat
every
eyes
fall
far
find
five
fly
for
four
friend
full
funny
give
go
goes
good
green
grow
have
he
hear
help
her
here
hold
how
I
into
is
know
like
little
live
long
look
make
many
me
my
never
new
no
now
of
off
one
open
or
our
out
over
own
pictures
play
pull
put
read
said
see
she
sing
small
some
starts
take
the
their
they
those
three
to
today
too
two
very
walk
was
watch
water
we
what
where
who
why
with
would
write
yellow
you

Decoding skills taught to date: consonants *m, s, c, t*; short *a*; consonant *n*; consonant *d*; consonant *p*; consonant *f*; short *i*; consonant *r*; consonant *h*; /z/ spelled *s*; consonant *b*; consonant *g* (hard); short *o*; consonant *l*; consonant *x*; inflection *-s;* short *e*; consonant *y*; consonant *w*; consonant *k*; consonant *v*; consonant *j*; short *u*; /kw/ spelled *qu*; consonant *z*; final consonants *ll*; final consonants *ss*; consonants *-ck*; final consonants *ff*; final consonants *zz*; blends with *r*; blends with *l*; blends with *s*; final blend *mp*; final blend *nt*; final blend *nd*; final blend *st*; digraph *th*; ending *-s*; ending *-es*; ending *-ed* /ĕd/; ending *-ed* /d/; ending *-ed* /t/; ending *-ing*; digraphs *ch, tch*; possessives with *'s*; digraph *sh*; digraph *wh*; digraph *ph*; contractions *'s, n't*; long *a* (CVC*e*); soft *c* /s/; /j/ spelled *g, dge*; long *i* (CVC*e*); digraphs *kn, gn*; digraph *wr*; digraph *mb*

DECODABLE WORDS

Target Skill: **digraph *mb***

Lamb	numb
limb	thumb

Previously Taught Skills

am	bump	fun	is	sit
and	can	get	like	take
back	fine	glad	Mom	up
big	fixes	help	on	with

SKILLS APPLIED IN WORDS IN STORY: consonants *m, s, c, t*; short *a*; consonant *n*; consonant *d*; consonant *p*; consonant *f*; short *i*; consonant *h*; /z/ spelled *s*; consonant *b*; consonant *g* (hard); short *o*; consonant *l*; consonant *x*; short *e*; consonant *w*; consonant *k*; short *u*; consonants *-ck*; blends with *l*; final blend *mp*; final blend *nd;* digraph *th*; ending *-es*; long *a* (CVCe); long *i* (CVCe); digraph *mb*

HIGH-FREQUENCY WORDS

a	I	my	to
go	me	the	too

Houghton Mifflin Harcourt

BOOK 111

Lamb and I

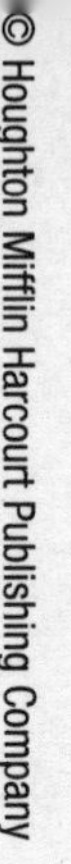

Ren Wren writes a lot.

Ben Wren has a pen.

Ben Wren writes a lot, too!

"Mom! Ben Wren wrecked it!"

Ren Wren Writes

Ren Wren has a pen.
Ren Wren writes.

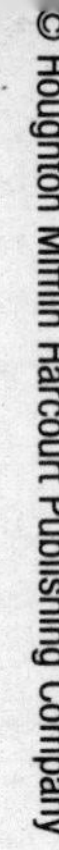

High-Frequency Words Taught to Date

a	cold	for	help	make	out	starts	watch
after	come	four	her	many	over	take	water
all	do	friend	here	me	own	the	we
and	does	full	hold	my	pictures	their	what
animal	down	funny	how	never	play	they	where
are	draw	give	I	new	pull	those	who
away	eat	go	into	no	put	three	why
be	every	goes	is	now	read	to	with
been	eyes	good	know	of	said	today	would
bird	fall	green	like	off	see	too	write
blue	far	grow	little	one	she	two	yellow
both	find	have	live	open	sing	very	you
brown	five	he	long	or	small	walk	
call	fly	hear	look	our	some	was	

Decoding skills taught to date: consonants *m, s, c, t*; short *a*; consonant *n*; consonant *d*; consonant *p*; consonant *f*; short *i*; consonant *r*; consonant *h*; /z/ spelled *s*; consonant *b*; consonant *g* (hard); short *o*; consonant *l*; consonant *x*; inflection *-s*; short *e*; consonant *y*; consonant *w*; consonant *k*; consonant *v*; consonant *j*; short *u*; /kw/ spelled *qu*; consonant *z*; final consonants *ll*; final consonants *ss*; consonants *ck*; final consonants *ff*; final consonants *zz*; blends with *r*; blends with *l*; blends with *s*; final blend *mp*; final blend *nt*; final blend *nd*; final blend *st*; digraph *th*; ending *-s*; ending *-es*; ending *-ed* /ed/; ending *-ed* /d/; ending *-ed* /t/; ending *-ing*; digraphs *ch, tch*; possessives with *'s*; digraph *sh*; digraph *wh*; digraph *ph*; contractions *'s, n't*; long *a* (CVC*e*); soft *c* /s/; /j/ spelled *g, dge*; long *i* (CVC*e*); digraphs *kn, gn*; digraph *wr*

Ren Wren Writes

DECODABLE WORDS

Target Skill: **digraph *wr***

wrecked writes

Wren

Previously Taught Skills

Ben lot Ren

has Mom

it pen

SKILLS APPLIED IN WORDS IN STORY: consonants *m, s, c, t*; short *a*; consonant *n*; consonant *p*; consonant *r*; consonant *h*; /z/ spelled *s*; consonant *b*; short *o*; consonant *l*; inflection *-s*; short *e*; consonant *w*; consonant *k*; consonants *ck*; blends with *r*; ending *-s*; long *i* (CVCe); digraphs *kn, gn* digraph *wr*

HIGH-FREQUENCY WORDS

a

too

Houghton Mifflin Harcourt

digraph *wr*

BOOK 110

Ren Wren Writes

Ren Wren cuts tape and wraps the box.

Ren Wren writes on a tag. It's time to give it to Ron!

Ron Wren likes the plane a lot.

Ren Wren Wraps

Ren Wren has a plane in a box.

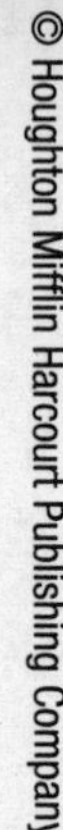

High-Frequency Words Taught to Date

Grade 1

a	cold	for	help	make	out	starts	watch
after	come	four	her	many	over	take	water
all	do	friend	here	me	own	the	we
and	does	full	hold	my	pictures	their	what
animal	down	funny	how	never	play	they	where
are	draw	give	I	new	pull	those	who
away	eat	go	into	no	put	three	why
be	every	goes	is	now	read	to	with
been	eyes	good	know	of	said	today	would
bird	fall	green	like	off	see	too	write
blue	far	grow	little	one	she	two	yellow
both	find	have	live	open	sing	very	you
brown	five	he	long	or	small	walk	
call	fly	hear	look	our	some	was	

Decoding skills taught to date: consonants *m, s, c, t*; short *a*; consonant *n*; consonant *d*; consonant *p*; consonant *f*; short *i*; consonant *r*; consonant *h*; /z/ spelled *s*; consonant *b*; consonant *g* (hard); short *o*; consonant *l*; consonant *x*; inflection *-s*; short *e*; consonant *y*; consonant *w*; consonant *k*; consonant *v*; consonant *j*; short *u*; /kw/ spelled *qu*; consonant *z*; final consonants *ll*; final consonants *ss*; consonants *ck*; final consonants *ff*; final consonants *zz*; blends with *r*; blends with *l*; blends with *s*; final blend *mp*; final blend *nt*; final blend *nd;* final blend *st*; digraph *th*; ending *-s*; ending *-es*; ending *-ed* /ed/; ending *-ed* /d/; ending *-ed* /t/; ending *-ing*; digraphs *ch, tch*; possessives with *'s*; digraph *sh*; digraph *wh*; digraph *ph*; contractions *'s, n't*; long *a* (CVC*e*); soft *c* /s/; /j/ spelled *g, dge;* long *i* (CVC*e*); digraphs *kn, gn*; digraph *wr*

Ren Wren Wraps

DECODABLE WORDS

Target Skill: **digraph *wr***

wraps Wren writes

Previously Taught Skills

and	has	likes	Ron
box	in	on	tag
cuts	it	plane	tape
give	it's	Ren	time

SKILLS APPLIED IN WORDS IN STORY: consonants *m, s, c, t*; short *a*; consonant *n*; consonant *p*; short *i*; consonant *r*; consonant *h*; /z/ spelled *s*; consonant *b*; consonant *g* (hard); short *o*; consonant *x*; inflection *-s*; short *e*; consonant *w*; consonant *k*; consonant *v*; short *u*; blends with *l*; final blend *-nd*; ending *-s*; contractions *'s, n't*; long *a* (CVC*e*); long *i* (CVC*e*)

HIGH-FREQUENCY WORDS

a the to

Houghton Mifflin Harcourt

digraph *wr*

BOOK 109

Ren Wren Wraps

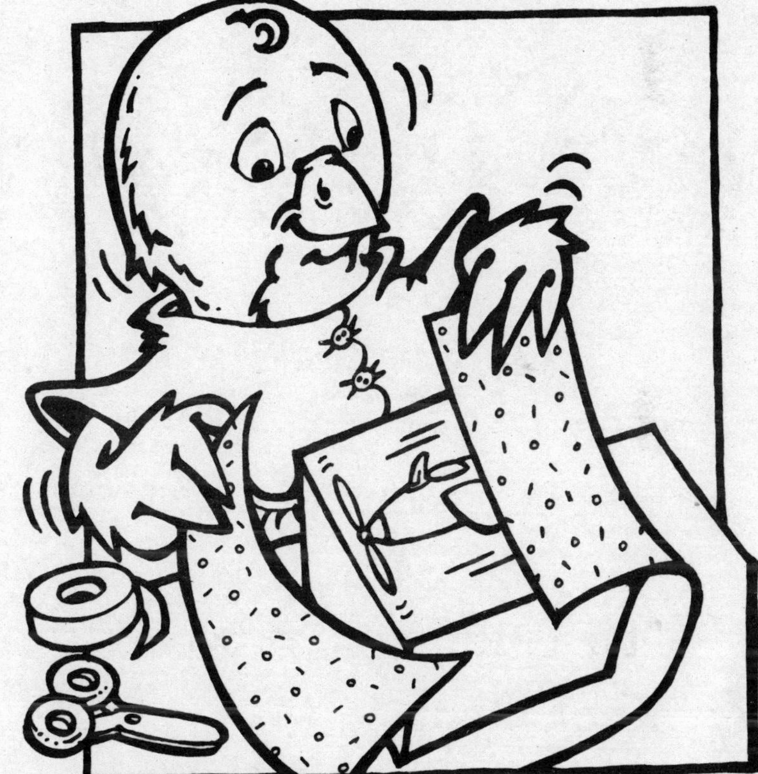

"Liz Gnat is on a trip!"
Knox Gnat sobs.

Knock! Knock!
Liz Gnat is back!

Knox Gnat is glad.

Knox Gnat

Knox Gnat is sad.

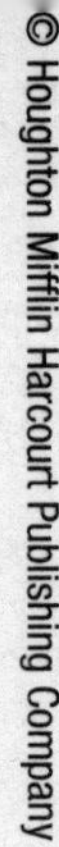

High-Frequency Words Taught to Date

a	cold	for	help	make	out	starts	watch
after	come	four	her	many	over	take	water
all	do	friend	here	me	own	the	we
and	does	full	hold	my	pictures	their	what
animal	down	funny	how	never	play	they	where
are	draw	give	I	new	pull	those	who
away	eat	go	into	no	put	three	why
be	every	goes	is	now	read	to	with
been	eyes	good	know	of	said	today	would
bird	fall	green	like	off	see	too	write
blue	far	grow	little	one	she	two	yellow
both	find	have	live	open	sing	very	you
brown	five	he	long	or	small	walk	
call	fly	hear	look	our	some	was	

Decoding skills taught to date: consonants *m, s, c, t*; short *a*; consonant *n*; consonant *d*; consonant *p*; consonant *f*; short *i*; consonant *r*; consonant *h*; /z/ spelled *s*; consonant *b*; consonant *g* (hard); short *o*; consonant *l*; consonant *x*; inflection *-s*; short *e*; consonant *y*; consonant *w*; consonant *k*; consonant *v*; consonant *j*; short *u*; /kw/ spelled *qu*; consonant *z*; final consonants *ll*; final consonants *ss*; consonants *ck*; final consonants *ff*; final consonants *zz*; blends with *r*; blends with *l*; blends with *s*; final blend *mp*; final blend *nt*; final blend *nd;* final blend *st*; digraph *th*; ending *-s*; ending *-es*; ending *-ed* /ed/; ending *-ed* /d/; ending *-ed* /t/; ending *-ing*; digraphs *ch, tch*; possessives with *'s*; digraph *sh*; digraph *wh*; digraph *ph*; contractions *'s, n't*; long *a* (CVC*e*); soft *c* /s/; /j/ spelled *g, dge*; long *i* (CVC*e*); digraphs *kn, gn*

Knox Gnat

DECODABLE WORDS

Target Skill: **digraphs *kn*, *gn***

Gnat	knock	Knox

Previously Taught Skills

back	is	on	sobs
glad	Liz	sad	trip

SKILLS APPLIED IN WORDS IN STORY: consonants *m, s, c, t*; short *a*; consonant *n*; consonant *d*; consonant *p*; short *i*; consonant *r*; /z/ spelled *s*; consonant *b*; consonant *g*; short *o*; consonant *l*; consonant *x*; inflection *-s*; consonant *k*; consonants *ck*; blends with *l*; ending *-s*

HIGH-FREQUENCY WORDS

a

Houghton Mifflin Harcourt

Knox Gnat

He can sign his name but
can he make a hat?
Yak gets a big knot.

Will Yak ever get the knack
of knitting?

Yes! Yak can knit.
Knit, knit, knit.

Can Yak Knit?

Can Yak knit?

High-Frequency Words Taught to Date

a	cold	for	help	make	out	starts	watch
after	come	four	her	many	over	take	water
all	do	friend	here	me	own	the	we
and	does	full	hold	my	pictures	their	what
animal	down	funny	how	never	play	they	where
are	draw	give	I	new	pull	those	who
away	eat	go	into	no	put	three	why
be	every	goes	is	now	read	to	with
been	eyes	good	know	of	said	today	would
bird	fall	green	like	off	see	too	write
blue	far	grow	little	one	she	two	yellow
both	find	have	live	open	sing	very	you
brown	five	he	long	or	small	walk	
call	fly	hear	look	our	some	was	

Decoding skills taught to date: consonants *m, s, c, t*; short *a*; consonant *n*; consonant *d*; consonant *p*; consonant *f*; short *i*; consonant *r*; consonant *h*; /z/ spelled *s*; consonant *b*; consonant *g* (hard); short *o*; consonant *l*; consonant *x*; inflection *-s*; short *e*; consonant *y*; consonant *w*; consonant *k*; consonant *v*; consonant *j*; short *u*; /kw/ spelled *qu*; consonant *z*; final consonants *ll*; final consonants *ss*; consonants *ck*; final consonants *ff*; final consonants *zz*; blends with *r*; blends with *l*; blends with *s*; final blend *mp*; final blend *nt*; final blend *nd*; final blend *st*; digraph *th*; ending *-s*; ending *-es*; ending *-ed* /ed/; ending *-ed* /d/; ending *-ed* /t/; ending *-ing*; digraphs *ch, tch*; possessives with *'s*; digraph *sh*; digraph *wh*; digraph *ph*; contractions *'s, n't*; long *a* (CVC*e*); soft *c* /s/; /j/ spelled *g, dge*; long *i* (CVC*e*); digraphs *kn, gn*

Can Yak Knit?

DECODABLE WORDS

Target Skill: **digraphs *kn*, *gn***

knack	knit	knitting	knot	sign

Previously Taught Skills

big	can	gets	his	Yak
but	get	hat	name	yes

SKILLS APPLIED IN WORDS IN STORY: consonants *m, s, c, t*; short *a*; consonant *n*; short *i*; consonant *h*; consonant *b*; consonant *g*; short *o*; inflection *-s;* short *e*; consonant *y*; consonant *k*; consonants *ck*; ending *-s*; ending *-ing*; long *a* (CVC*e*)

HIGH-FREQUENCY WORDS

a	he	of
ever	make	the

Houghton Mifflin Harcourt

digraphs *kn*, *gn*

BOOK 107

Can Yak Knit?

Spice on rice is fine.
Lime on rice is nice, too.

"We can ride bikes," said Mike.
Mike got his new red bike, and
I got mine.

"We can ride on the slide," said Mike. Mike and I had a fun time.

My Pal Mike

I had lunch with my pal Mike. I had a bite of rice with spice and lime.

High-Frequency Words Taught to Date

a	cold	for	help	make	out	starts	watch
after	come	four	her	many	over	take	water
all	do	friend	here	me	own	the	we
and	does	full	hold	my	pictures	their	what
animal	down	funny	how	never	play	they	where
are	draw	give	I	new	pull	those	who
away	eat	go	into	no	put	three	why
be	every	goes	is	now	read	to	with
been	eyes	good	know	of	said	today	would
bird	fall	green	like	off	see	too	write
blue	far	grow	little	one	she	two	yellow
both	find	have	live	open	sing	very	you
brown	five	he	long	or	small	walk	
call	fly	hear	look	our	some	was	

Decoding skills taught to date: consonants *m, s, c, t*; short *a*; consonant *n*; consonant *d*; consonant *p*; consonant *f*; short *i*; consonant *r*; consonant *h*; /z/ spelled *s*; consonant *b*; consonant *g* (hard); short *o*; consonant *l*; consonant *x*; inflection *-s*; short *e*; consonant *y*; consonant *w*; consonant *k*; consonant *v*; consonant *j*; short *u*; /kw/ spelled *qu*; consonant *z*; final consonants *ll*; final consonants *ss*; consonants *ck*; final consonants *ff*; final consonants *zz*; blends with *r*; blends with *l*; blends with *s*; final blend *mp*; final blend *nt*; final blend *nd*; final blend *st*; digraph *th*; ending *-s*; ending *-es*; ending *-ed* /ed/; ending *-ed* /d/; ending *-ed* /t/; ending *-ing*; digraphs *ch, tch*; possessives with *'s*; digraph *sh*; digraph *wh*; digraph *ph*; contractions *'s, n't*; long *a* (CVC*e*); soft *c* /s/; /j/ spelled *g, dge*; long *i* (CVC*e*)

My Pal Mike

DECODABLE WORDS

Target Skill: **long *i* (CVC*e*)**

bike	fine	Mike	rice	spice
bikes	like	mine	ride	time
bite	lime	nice	slide	

Previously Taught Skills

and	got	is	pal
can	had	lunch	red
fun	his	new	with

SKILLS APPLIED IN WORDS IN STORY: consonants *m, s, c, t*; short *a*; consonant *n*; consonant *d*; consonant *p*; consonant *f*; short *i*; consonant *r*; consonant *h*; /z/ spelled *s*; consonant *b*; consonant *g*; short *o*; consonant *l*; inflection *-s*; consonant *w*; consonant *k*; short *u*; blends with *l*; blends with *s*; final blend *nd*; digraph *th*; ending *-s*; digraphs *ch, tch*; contractions *'s, n't*; soft *c* /s/

HIGH-FREQUENCY WORDS

a	of	too
I	said	we
my	the	

Houghton Mifflin Harcourt

long *i* (CVC*e*)

BOOK 106

My Pal Mike

The white mice slide on ice.
Slide, mice, slide!

The white mice take a drive.
Drive, mice, drive!

The white mice had a nice time!

White Mice

The white mice ride bikes.

Ride, mice, ride!

High-Frequency Words Taught to Date

a	cold	for	help	make	out	starts	watch
after	come	four	her	many	over	take	water
all	do	friend	here	me	own	the	we
and	does	full	hold	my	pictures	their	what
animal	down	funny	how	never	play	they	where
are	draw	give	I	new	pull	those	who
away	eat	go	into	no	put	three	why
be	every	goes	is	now	read	to	with
been	eyes	good	know	of	said	today	would
bird	fall	green	like	off	see	too	write
blue	far	grow	little	one	she	two	yellow
both	find	have	live	open	sing	very	you
brown	five	he	long	or	small	walk	
call	fly	hear	look	our	some	was	

Decoding skills taught to date: consonants *m, s, c, t*; short *a*; consonant *n*; consonant *d*; consonant *p*; consonant *f*; short *i*; consonant *r*; consonant *h*; /z/ spelled *s*; consonant *b*; consonant *g*; short *o*; consonant *l*; consonant *x*; inflection *-s*; short *e*; consonant *y*; consonant *w*; consonant *k*; consonant *v*; consonant *j*; short *u*; /kw/ spelled *qu*; consonant *z*; final consonants *ll*; final consonants *ss*; consonants *ck*; final consonants *ff*; final consonants *zz*; blends with *r*; blends with *l*; blends with *s*; final blend *mp*; final blend *nt*; final blend *nd*; final blend *st*; digraph *th*; ending *-s*; ending *-es*; ending *-ed* /ed/; ending *-ed* /d/; ending *-ed* /t/; ending *-ing*; digraphs *ch, tch*; possessives with *'s*; digraph *sh*; digraph *wh*; digraph *ph*; contractions *'s, n't*; long *a* (CVC*e*); soft *c* /s/; /j/ spelled *g, dge;* long *i* (CVC*e*)

White Mice

DECODABLE WORDS

Target Skill: **long *i* (CVC*e*)**

bikes	ice	nice	slide	white
drive	mice	ride	time	

Previously Taught Skills

had

on

take

SKILLS APPLIED IN WORDS IN STORY: consonants *m, s, c, t*; short *a*; consonant *n*; consonant *d*; consonant *r*; consonant *h*; consonant *b*; consonant *l*; inflection -*s*; consonant *w*; consonant *k*; consonant *v*; blends with *r*; blends with *l*; blends with *s*; ending -*s*; digraph *wh*; soft *c* /s/

HIGH-FREQUENCY WORDS

a the

Houghton Mifflin Harcourt.

long *i* (CVC*e*)

BOOK 105

White Mice

Jake and Dad cut a wedge of fudge cake for the fudge judge.

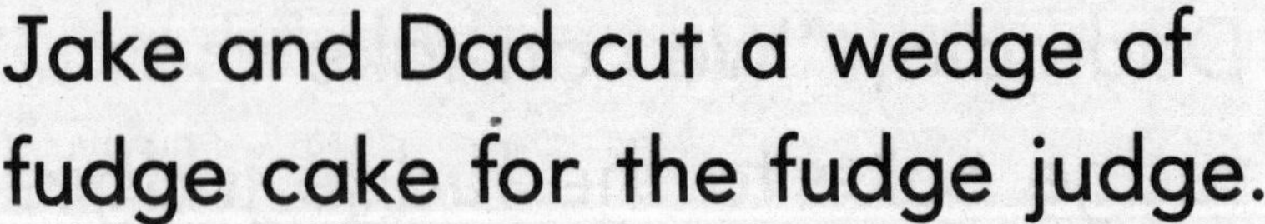

Page, the fudge judge, had the fudge cakes. Then, Page had Jake's fudge cake.

Page, the fudge judge, said,
"Jake's fudge cake is best!
Jake wins the badge!"

The Fudge Judge

Jake baked a fudge cake.
Dad said, "We can take the
fudge cake to the fudge judge.
The best fudge cake will win
a badge."

High-Frequency Words Taught to Date

a	draw	grow	make	play	today
after	eat	have	many	pull	too
all	every	he	me	put	two
and	fall	hear	my	read	very
animal	far	help	never	said	was
are	find	her	new	see	watch
away	five	here	no	she	water
be	for	hold	now	sing	we
been	four	how	of	small	what
blue	friend	I	off	some	where
brown	full	into	one	starts	who
call	funny	is	open	take	why
cold	give	know	our	the	with
come	go	like	out	their	would
do	goes	little	over	they	write
does	good	live	own	three	yellow
down	green	look	pictures	to	you

Decoding skills taught to date: consonants *m, s, c, t*; short *a*; consonant *n*; consonant *d*; consonant *p*; consonant *f*; short *i*; consonant *r*; consonant *h*; /z/ spelled *s*; consonant *b*; consonant *g* (hard); short *o*; consonant *l*; consonant *x*, inflection *-s*; short *e*; consonant *y*; consonant *w*; consonant *k*; consonant *v*; consonant *j*; short *u*; /kw/ spelled *qu*; consonant *z*; final consonants *ll*; final consonants *ss*; consonants *ck*; final consonants *ff*; final consonants *zz*; blends with *r*; blends with *l*; blends with *s*; final blend *mp*; final blend *nt*; final blend *nd*; final blend *st*; digraph *th*; ending *-s*; ending *-es*; ending *-ed* /ed/; ending *-ed* /d/; ending *-ed* /t/; ending *-ing*; digraphs *ch, tch*; possessives with *'s*; digraph *sh*; digraph *wh*; digraph *ph*; contractions *'s, n't*; long *a* (CVC*e*); soft *c* /s/; /j/ spelled *g, dge*

The Fudge Judge

DECODABLE WORDS

Target Skill: /j/ spelled *g, dge*

badge	judge	wedge
fudge	Page	

Previously Taught Skills

and	cakes	had	take
baked	can	is	will
best	cut	Jake	win
cake	Dad	Jake's	wins

SKILLS APPLIED IN WORDS IN STORY: consonants *s, c, t*; short *a*; consonant *n*; consonant *d*; consonant *p*; consonant *f*; short *i*; /z/ spelled *s*; consonant *b*; consonant *l*; inflection *-s*; short *e*; consonant *w*; consonant *k*; consonant *j*; short *u*; final consonants *ll*; blends with *s*; final blend *nd*; final blend *st*; ending *-s*; ending *-ed* /t/; possessives with *'s*; long *a* (CVCe)

HIGH-FREQUENCY WORDS

a	of	the	we
for	said	to	

Houghton Mifflin Harcourt

/j/ spelled *g, dge*

BOOK 104

The Fudge Judge

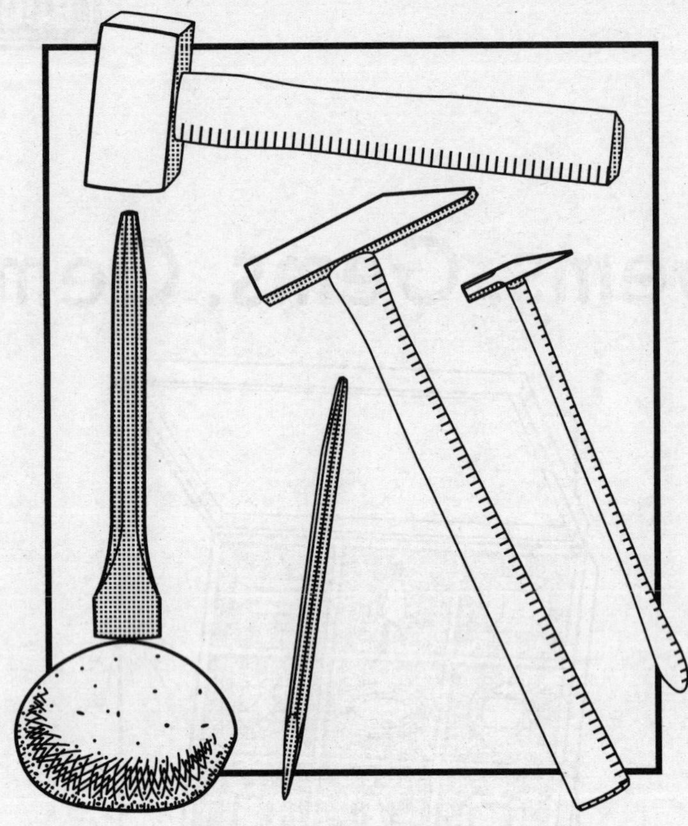

We can get gems in cliffs and rock ledges. We must chip away at rocks to get gems.

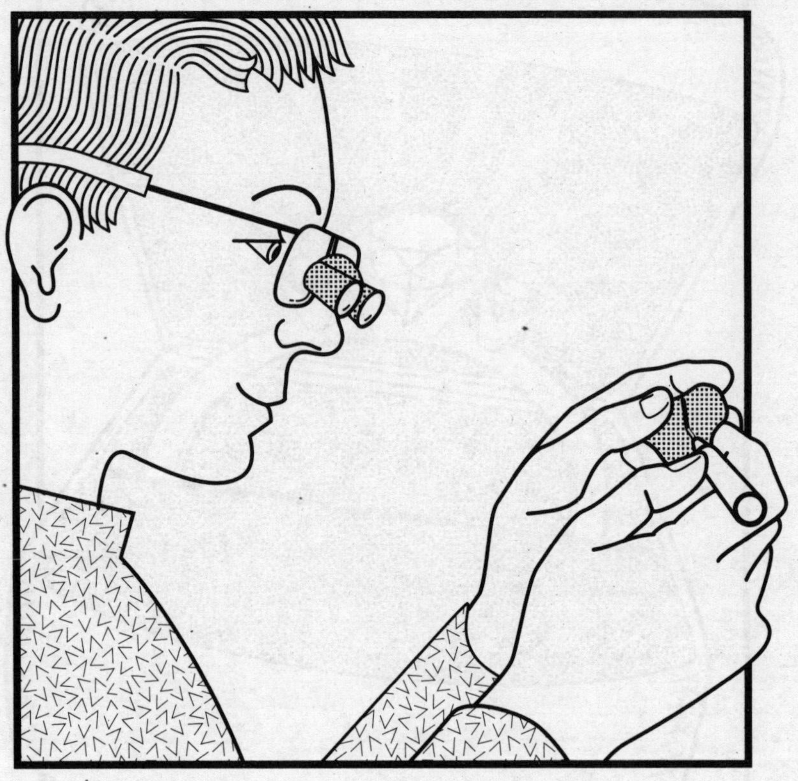

Dodge will cut the big gem. That is his job. Dodge will cut edges and ridges. The edges will make the gem flash.

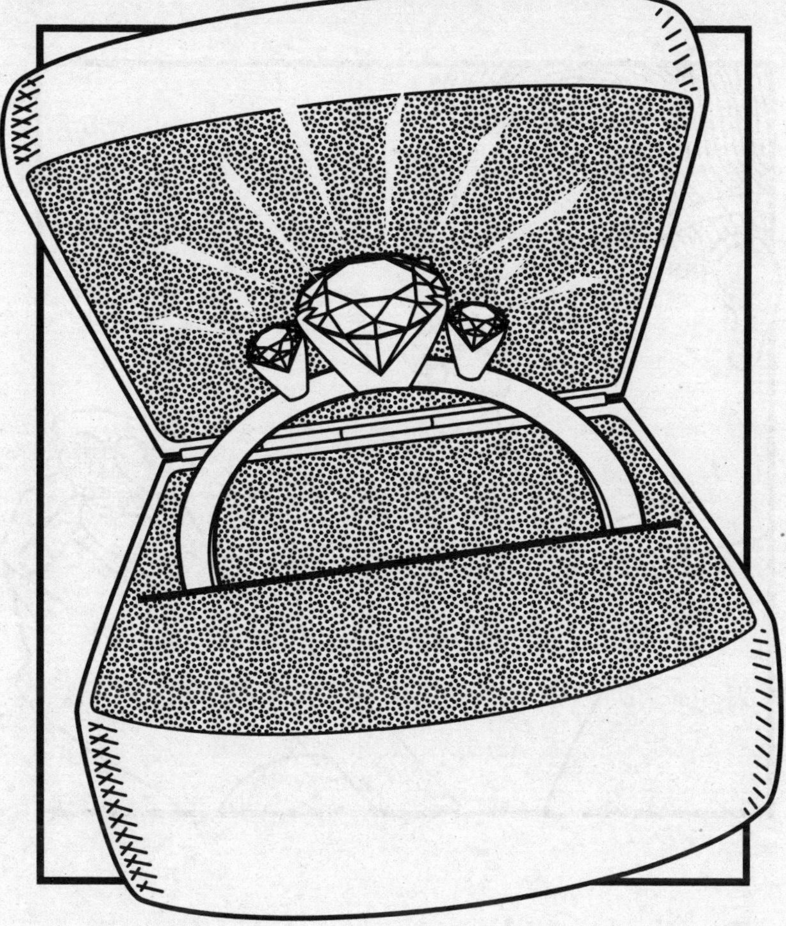

Dodge sets gems in a band. Gems glint in the band. It will look good on a hand.

Gems, Gems, Gems

Gems have many shapes. Gems can flash and glint.

High-Frequency Words Taught to Date

a	draw	grow	make	play	today
after	eat	have	many	pull	too
all	every	he	me	put	two
and	fall	hear	my	read	very
animal	far	help	never	said	was
are	find	her	new	see	watch
away	five	here	no	she	water
be	for	hold	now	sing	we
been	four	how	of	small	what
blue	friend	I	off	some	where
brown	full	into	one	starts	who
call	funny	is	open	take	why
cold	give	know	our	the	with
come	go	like	out	their	would
do	goes	little	over	they	write
does	good	live	own	three	yellow
down	green	look	pictures	to	you

Decoding skills taught to date: consonants *m, s, c, t*; short *a*; consonant *n*; consonant *d*; consonant *p*; consonant *f*; short *i*; consonant *r*; consonant *h*; /z/ spelled *s*; consonant *b*; consonant *g* (hard); short *o*; consonant *l*; consonant *x*; inflection *-s*; short *e*; consonant *y*; consonant *w*; consonant *k*; consonant *v*; consonant *j*; short *u*; /kw/ spelled *qu*; consonant *z*; final consonants *ll*; final consonants *ss*; consonants *ck*; final consonants *ff*; final consonants *zz*; blends with *r*; blends with *l*; blends with *s*; final blend *mp*; final blend *nt*; final blend *nd*; final blend *st*; digraph *th*; ending *-s*; ending *-es*; ending *-ed* /ed/; ending *-ed* /d/; ending *-ed* /t/; ending *-ing*; digraphs *ch, tch*; possessives with *'s*; digraph *sh*; digraph *wh*; digraph *ph*; contractions *'s, n't*; long *a* (CVC*e*); soft *c* /s/; /j/ spelled *g, dge*

Gems, Gems, Gems

DECODABLE WORDS

Target Skill: **/j/ spelled *g, dge***

Dodge	gem	ledges
edges	gems	ridges

Previously Taught Skills

and	chip	hand	job	rocks
at	cut	his	make	sets
band	flash	in	must	shapes
big	get	is	on	that
can	glint	it	rock	will

SKILLS APPLIED IN WORDS IN STORY: consonants *m, s, c, t*; short *a*; consonant *n*; consonant *d*; consonant *p*; consonant *f*; short *i*; consonant *r*; consonant *h*; /z/ spelled *s*; consonant *b*; consonant *g* (hard); short *o*; consonant *l*; inflection *-s*; short *e*; consonant *w*; final consonants *ll*; consonants *ck*; blends with *l*; blends with *s*; final blend *nd;* final blend *st*; digraph *th*; ending *-s*; digraphs *ch, tch*; digraph *sh*; long *a* (CVCe)

HIGH-FREQUENCY WORDS

a	good	look	to
are	have	many	we
away	here	the	

Houghton Mifflin Harcourt

/j/ spelled *g, dge*

BOOK 103

Gems, Gems, Gems

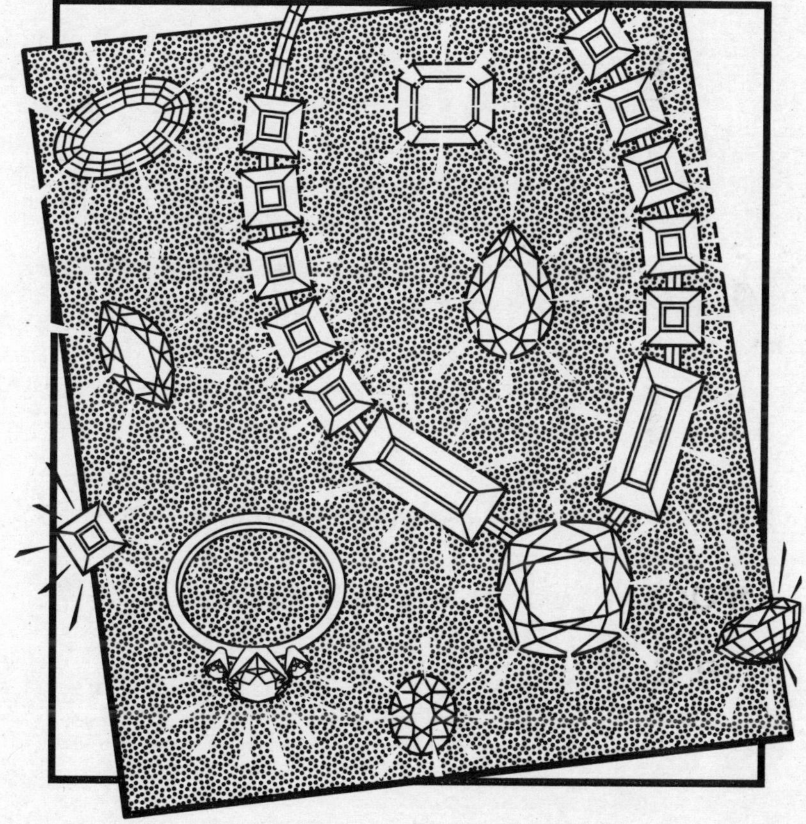

Grace's snacks will not sell.
Grace said, "Now snacks cost
five cents."

Grace's snacks still will not sell.
Grace's face is sad. "Is this not
a good space?" said Grace.

Grace set her snacks in a new place. Now Grace's snacks sell, sell, sell!

Space for Grace

Grace has a glad face. Grace and her dog Ace will sell snacks. Grace's snacks cost ten cents.

High-Frequency Words Taught to Date

Grade 1

a	draw	grow	make	play	today
after	eat	have	many	pull	too
all	every	he	me	put	two
and	fall	hear	my	read	very
animal	far	help	never	said	was
are	find	her	new	see	watch
away	five	here	no	she	water
be	for	hold	now	sing	we
been	four	how	of	small	what
blue	friend	I	off	some	where
brown	full	into	one	starts	who
call	funny	is	open	take	why
cold	give	know	our	the	with
come	go	like	out	their	would
do	goes	little	over	they	write
does	good	live	own	three	yellow
down	green	look	pictures	to	you

Decoding skills taught to date: consonants *m, s, c, t*; short *a*; consonant *n*; consonant *d*; consonant *p*; consonant *f*; short *i*; consonant *r*; consonant *h*; /z/ spelled *s*; consonant *b*; consonant *g*; short *o*; consonant *l*; consonant *x*; inflection *-s*; short *e*; consonant *y*; consonant *w*; consonant *k*; consonant *v*; consonant *j*; short *u*; /kw/ spelled *qu*; consonant *z*; final consonants *ll*; final consonants *ss*; consonants *ck*; final consonants *ff*; final consonants *zz*; blends with *r*; blends with *l*; blends with *s*; final blend *mp*; final blend *nt*; final blend *nd*; final blend *st*; digraph *th*; ending *-s*; ending *-es*; ending *-ed* /ed/; ending *-ed* /d/; base words and ending *-ed* /t/; ending *-ing*; digraphs *ch, tch*; possessives with *'s*; digraph *sh*; digraph *wh*; digraph *ph*; contractions *'s, n't*; long *a* (CVC*e*); soft *c* /s/

Space for Grace

DECODABLE WORDS

Target Skill: **soft c /s/**

Ace	face	Grace's	space
cents	Grace	place	

Previously Taught Skills

and	has	sad	still
cost	in	sell	ten
dog	is	set	this
glad	not	snacks	will

SKILLS APPLIED IN WORDS IN STORY: consonants *m, s, c, t*; short *a*; consonant *n*; consonant *d*; consonant *p*; consonant *f*; short *i*; consonant *r*; consonant *h*; /z/ spelled *s*; consonant *g*; short *o*; consonant *l*; inflection *-s*; short *e*; consonant *w*; final consonants *ll*; consonants *ck*; blends with *r*; blends with *l*; blends with *s*; final blend *nd*; digraph *th*; ending *-s*; possessives with *'s*; long *a* (CVC*e*)

HIGH-FREQUENCY WORDS

a	good	now
five	her	said
for	new	

Houghton Mifflin Harcourt

soft c /s/

BOOK 102

Space for Grace

The race is on!
Run, Vince!
Vince is fast. Will Vince win the race?

Here is Vance. Run, Vance!
Vance runs with such grace.
Can Vance win the race?

Vance wins the race!
Vince calls to Vance,
"Good race!"

soft *c* /s/

A Race

Vince and Vance will race.

High-Frequency Words Taught to Date

Grade 1

a	draw	grow	make	play	today
after	eat	have	many	pull	too
all	every	he	me	put	two
and	fall	hear	my	read	very
animal	far	help	never	said	was
are	find	her	new	see	watch
away	five	here	no	she	water
be	for	hold	now	sing	we
been	four	how	of	small	what
blue	friend	I	off	some	where
brown	full	into	one	starts	who
call	funny	is	open	take	why
cold	give	know	our	the	with
come	go	like	out	their	would
do	goes	little	over	they	write
does	good	live	own	three	yellow
down	green	look	pictures	to	you

Decoding skills taught to date: consonants *m, s, c, t*; short *a*; consonant *n*; consonant *d*; consonant *p*; consonant *f*; short *i*; consonant *r*; consonant *h*; /z/ spelled *s*; consonant *b*; consonant *g*; short *o*; consonant *l*; consonant *x*; inflection *-s*; short *e*; consonant *y*; consonant *w*; consonant *k*; consonant *v*; consonant *j*; short *u*; /kw/ spelled *qu*; consonant *z*; final consonants *ll*; final consonants *ss*; consonants *ck*; final consonants *ff*; final consonants *zz*; blends with *r*; blends with *l*; blends with *s*; final blend *mp*; final blend *nt*; final blend *nd*; final blend *st*; digraph *th*; ending *-s*; ending *-es*; ending *-ed* /ed/; ending *-ed* /d/; ending *-ed* /t/; ending *-ing*; digraphs *ch*, *tch*; possessives with *'s*; digraph *sh*; digraph *wh*; digraph *ph*; contractions *'s*, *n't*; long *a* (CVC*e*); soft *c* /s/

A Race

DECODABLE WORDS

Target Skill: **soft *c* /s/**

grace Vance
race Vince

Previously Taught Skills

and	is	runs	win
can	on	such	wins
fast	run	will	

SKILLS APPLIED IN WORDS IN STORY: consonants *m, s, c, t*; short *a*; consonant *n*; consonant *f*; short *i*; consonant *r*; /z/ spelled *s*; consonant *g*; short *o*; consonant *l*; inflection -*s*; consonant *w*; consonant *v*; short *u*; final consonants *ll*; blends with *r*; digraph *th*; ending -*s*; digraphs *ch, tch*; long *a* (CVCe)

HIGH-FREQUENCY WORDS

a	here	with
calls	the	
good	to	

Houghton Mifflin Harcourt.

soft *c* /s/

BOOK 101

A Race

Tate's mom is named Jade.
Jade gave Tate a shake.
Wake up, Tate!

Tate's dad is named Zane.
Zane has a thick mane.

It is not safe to pet Tate,
Jade, and Zane.
They are not tame.

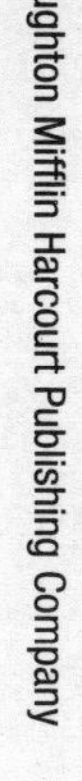

Tate, Jade, and Zane

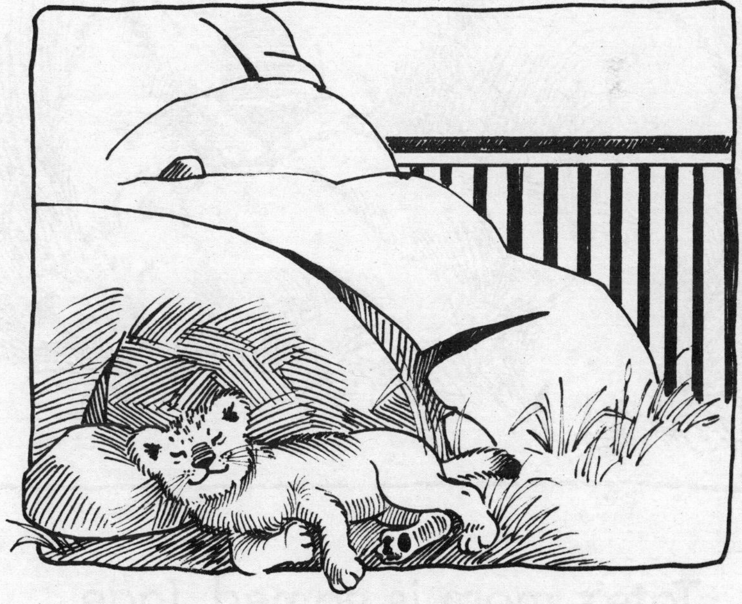

A cub naps in the shade.
His name is Tate.

High-Frequency Words Taught to Date

a
after
all
and
animal
are
away
be
been
blue
brown
call
cold
come
do
does
down
draw
eat
every
fall
far
find
five
for
four
friend
full
funny
give
go
goes
good
green
grow
have
he
hear
help
her
here
hold
how
I
into
is
know
like
little
live
look
make
many
me
my
never
new
no
now
of
off
one
open
our
out
over
own
pictures
play
pull
put
read
said
see
she
sing
small
some
starts
take
the
their
they
three
to
today
too
two
very
was
watch
water
we
what
where
who
why
with
would
write
yellow
you

Decoding skills taught to date: consonants *m, s, c, t*; short *a*; consonant *n*; consonant *d*; consonant *p*; consonant *f*; short *i*; consonant *r*; consonant *h*; /z/ spelled *s*; consonant *b*; consonant *g*; short *o*; consonant *l*; consonant *x*; inflection *-s*; short *e*; consonant *y*; consonant *w*; consonant *k*; consonant *v*; consonant *j*; short *u*; /kw/ spelled *qu*; consonant *z*; final consonants *ll*; final consonants *ss*; consonants *-ck*; final consonants *ff*; final consonants *zz*; blends with *r*; blends with *l*; blends with *s*; final blend *mp*; final blend *nt*; final blend *nd*; final blend *st*; digraph *th*; ending *-s*; ending *-es*; ending *-ed* /ed/; ending *-ed* /d/; ending *-ed* /t/; ending *-ing*; digraphs *ch, tch*; possessives with *'s*; digraph *sh*; digraph *wh*; digraph *ph*; contractions *'s, n't*; long *a* (CVC*e*)

Tate, Jade, and Zane

DECODABLE WORDS

Target Skill: **long *a* (CVC*e*)**

gave	named	shake	Tate's
Jade	safe	tame	wake
name	shade	Tate	Zane

Previously Taught Skills

and	has	is	naps	up
cub	his	it	pet	
dad	in	mom	thick	

SKILLS APPLIED IN WORDS IN STORY: consonants *m, s, c, t*; short *a*; consonant *n*; consonant *d*; consonant *p*; short *i*; consonant *h*; /z/ spelled *s*; consonant *b*; consonant *g*; short *o*; inflection -*s*; short *e*; consonant *w*; consonant *k*; consonant *v*; consonant *j*; short *u*; consonant *z*; consonants -*ck*; blends with *s*; final blend *nd*; digraph *th*; ending -*s*; ending -*ed* /d/; possessives with *'s*; digraph *sh*; long *a* (CVCe)

HIGH-FREQUENCY WORDS

a	the	to
are	they	

Houghton Mifflin Harcourt

long *a* (CVC*e*)

BOOK 100

Tate, Jade, and Zane

Nate writes the date.
Nate writes his name.
Kate makes shapes with blocks.
It is a fun math game.

Nate and Kate draw a lake.
Miss Bates will tape it up.

Nate and Kate wave at the gate.
Kate gets on the bus.

Nate and Kate

Nate is in first grade. Kate is in first grade, too. Nate and Kate sit in the same class.

High-Frequency Words Taught to Date

a	come	friend	her	many	over	starts	water
after	do	full	here	me	own	take	we
all	does	funny	hold	my	pictures	the	what
and	down	give	how	never	play	their	where
animal	draw	go	I	new	pull	they	who
are	eat	goes	into	no	put	three	why
away	every	good	is	now	read	to	with
be	fall	green	know	of	said	today	would
been	far	grow	like	off	see	too	write
blue	find	have	little	one	she	two	yellow
brown	five	he	live	open	sing	very	you
call	for	hear	look	our	small	was	
cold	four	help	make	out	some	watch	

Decoding skills taught to date: consonants *m, s, c, t*; short *a*; consonant *n*; consonant *d*; consonant *p*; consonant *f*; short *i*; consonant *r*; consonant *h*; /z/ spelled *s*; consonant *b*; consonant *g*; short *o*; consonant *l*; consonant *x*; inflection *-s*; short *e*; consonant *y*; consonant *w*; consonant *k*; consonant *v*; consonant *j*; short *u*; /kw/ spelled *qu*; consonant *z*; final consonants *ll*; final consonants *ss*; consonants *ck*; final consonants *ff*; final consonants *zz*; blends with *r*; blends with *l*; blends with *s*; final blend *mp*; final blend *nt*; final blend *nd*; final blend *st*; digraph *th*; ending *-s*; ending *-es*; ending *-ed* /ed/; ending *-ed* /d/; ending *-ed* /t/; ending *-ing*; digraphs *ch, tch*; possessives with *'s*; digraph *sh*; digraph *wh*; digraph *ph*; contractions *'s, n't*; long *a* (CVC*e*)

Nate and Kate

DECODABLE WORDS

Target Skill: **long *a* (CVC*e*)**

Bates	grade	makes	same	wave
date	Kate	name	shapes	
gate	lake	Nate	tape	

Previously Taught Skills

and	game	is	on	with
at	gets	it	sit	
class	his	math	up	
fun	in	Miss	will	

SKILLS APPLIED IN WORDS IN STORY: consonants *m, s, c, t*; short *a*; consonant *n*; consonant *d*; consonant *p*; consonant *f*; short *i*; consonant *r*; consonant *h*; /z/ spelled *s*; consonant *b*; consonant *g* (hard); short *o*; consonant *l*; inflection *-s*; consonant *w*; consonant *k*; consonant *v*; short *u*; final consonants *ll*; final consonants *ss*; blends with *r*; blends with *s*; final blend *nd*; digraph *th*; ending *-s*; ending *-es*; digraph *sh*; long *a* (CVC*e*)

HIGH-FREQUENCY WORDS

a	first	too
draw	the	write(s)

Houghton Mifflin Harcourt

long *a* (CVC*e*)

BOOK 99

Nate and Kate

"We will help you get rid of Fox,"
Dog said. Then Dog got Hen off
the hut.
"When Fox comes, ask him in,"
said Duck.

"Come in, Fox," said Hen.
Fox licked his lips.
Then Bat buzzed him. Dog
jumped on him. Duck bit him.

"Help!" yelled Fox.
Fox ran and ran and didn't stop.
"You got rid of Fox!" yelled
Hen. "I am glad!"

Get Rid of Fox

Duck, Dog, and Bat went to Hen's
hut. Hen sat on top of her hut.
"Why are you on top?" said Duck.
"It's Fox. He is at this hut a lot.
I can't let him get me," said Hen.

High-Frequency Words Taught to Date

Grade 1

a	cold	friend	help	make	our	small	we
after	come	full	her	many	out	some	what
all	do	funny	here	me	own	take	where
and	does	give	hold	my	pictures	the	who
animal	down	green	how	never	play	their	why
are	draw	go	I	new	pull	they	with
away	eat	goes	is	no	put	to	would
be	every	good	know	now	read	today	write
been	fall	grow	like	of	said	too	yellow
blue	far	have	little	off	see	very	you
brown	find	he	live	one	she	was	
call	for	hear	look	open	sing	water	

Decoding skills taught to date: consonants *m, s, t, c*; short *a*; consonant *n*; consonant *d*; consonant *p*; consonant *f*; short *i*; consonant *r*; consonant *h*; consonant *s* /z/; consonant *b*; consonant *g* (hard); short *o*; consonant *l*; consonant *x*; inflection *-s*; short *e*; consonant *y*; consonant *w*; consonant *k*; consonant *v*; consonant *j*; short *u*; consonant *qu*; consonant *z*; double final consonants *ll*; double final consonants *ss*; consonants *-ck*; double final consonants *ff*; double final consonants *zz*; blends with *r*; blends with *l*; blends with *s*; final blend *mp*; final blend *nt*; final blend *nd*; final blend *st*; digraph *th*; base words and ending *-s*; base words and ending *-es*; base words and ending *-ed* /ed/; base words and ending -ed /d/; base words and ending *-ed* /t/; base words and ending *-ing*; digraphs *ch, tch*; possessives with *'s*; digraph *sh*; digraph *wh*; digraph *ph*; contractions with *'s* and *n't*

Get Rid of Fox

DECODABLE WORDS

Target Skill: **contractions with *'s* and *n't***

can't	didn't	it's		

Previously Taught Skills

am	Fox	hut	on	up
and	get	in	ran	went
ask	glad	is	rid	when
at	got	jumped	sat	will
bit	Hen	let	stop	yelled
buzzed	Hen's	licked	then	
Dog	him	lips	this	
Duck	his	lot	top	

SKILLS APPLIED IN WORDS IN STORY: consonants *m, s, t, c*; short *a*; consonant *n*; consonant *d*; consonant *p*; consonant *f*; short *i*; consonant *r*; consonant *h*; consonant *s* /z/; consonant *b*; consonant *g* (hard); short *o*; consonant *l*; consonant *x*; inflection *-s*; short *e*; consonant *y;* consonant *w*; consonant *j*; short *u*; consonant *z*; double final consonants *ll*; double final consonants *ff*; double final consonants *zz*; blends with *s*; final blend *mp*; final blend *nd;* digraph *th*; base words and ending *-s*; base words and ending *-ed* /d/; base words and ending *-ed* /t/; possessives with *'s*; digraph *wh*; contractions with *'s* and *n't*

HIGH-FREQUENCY WORDS

a	he	me	the	you
are	help	of	to	
come	her	off	we	
comes	I	said	why	

Houghton Mifflin Harcourt

contractions *'s, n't*

BOOK 98

Get Rid of Fox

"It thumps," said Lon.
"It's a truck, isn't it!"
"That's not a truck," said his dad.
"Not yet!"

"Well, it isn't a bat!" said Lon.
"This box will not fit a big bat."
"Open it up," said his dad.

"Yes!" said Lon. "It's a kit!
It **makes** a truck!"

Not Yet

Lon looked at the box.
"What is it?" he asked.
"It's for you," said his dad.
"Pick it up, Lon."

High-Frequency Words Taught to Date

Grade 1

a	cold	friend	help	make	our	small	we
after	come	full	her	many	out	some	what
all	do	funny	here	me	own	take	where
and	does	give	hold	my	pictures	the	who
animal	down	go	how	never	play	their	why
are	draw	goes	I	new	pull	they	with
away	eat	good	is	no	put	to	would
be	every	green	know	now	read	today	write
been	fall	grow	like	of	said	too	yellow
blue	far	have	little	off	see	very	you
brown	find	he	live	one	she	was	
call	for	hear	look	open	sing	water	

Decoding skills taught to date: consonants *m, s, t,* c; short *a*; consonant *n*; consonant *d*; consonant *p*; consonant *f*, short *i*; consonant *r*, consonant *h*; consonant *s* /z/; consonant *b*; consonant *g* (hard); short *o*; consonant *l*; consonant *x*; inflection *-s*; short *e*; consonant *y*, consonant *w*; consonant *k*; consonant *v*; consonant *j*; short *u*; consonants *qu*; consonant *z*; double final consonants *ll*; double final consonants *ss*; consonants *ck*; double final consonants *ff*; double final consonants *zz*; blends with *r*; blends with *l*; blends with *s*; final blend *mp*; final blend *nt*; final blend *nd*; final blend *st*; digraph *th*; base words and ending *-s*; base words and ending *-es*; base words and ending *-ed* /ed/; base words and ending *-ed* /d/; base words and ending *-ed* /t/; base words and ending *-ing*; digraphs *ch, tch*; possessives with *'s*; digraph *sh*; digraph *wh;* digraph *ph*; contractions *'s* and *n't*

Not Yet

DECODABLE WORDS

Target Skill: **contractions *'s, n't***

isn't	it's	that's

Previously Taught Skills

asked	dad	kit	truck	yet
at	his	Lon	up	
bat	in	not	well	
big	is	pick	will	
box	it	thumps	yes	

SKILLS APPLIED IN WORDS IN STORY: consonants *m, s, t, c*; short *a*; consonant *n*; consonant *d*; consonant *p*; short *i*; consonant *h*; /z/ spelled *s*; consonant *b*; consonant *g* (hard); short *o*; consonant *l*; consonant *x*; inflection *-s*; short *e*; consonant *y*; consonant *w*; consonant *k*; short *u*; double final consonants *ll*; consonants *ck*; blends with *r*; blends with *s*; base words and ending *-s*; final blend *mp*; base words and ending *-es*; base words and ending *-ed* /t/

HIGH-FREQUENCY WORDS

a	he	make(s)	said	what
for	look(ed)	open	the	you

Houghton Mifflin Harcourt

Not Yet

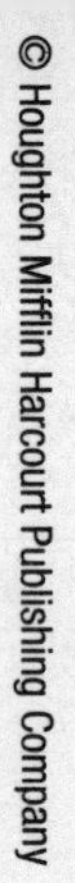

Ralph's class grows plants.
"How big is this plant today?"
asked Ralph.
"Too big for its pot!" said Phil.
Ralph logs it in his graph.

Ralph gets new pens. His
new graph will be red,
black, and blue.

Ralph is the graph man.

The Graph Man

Ralph's Green Club fills bags with cans. Ralph makes a graph as the bags fill up. Ralph likes graphs.

High-Frequency Words Taught to Date

Grade 1

a	cold	friend	help	make	our	small	we
after	come	full	her	many	out	some	what
all	do	funny	here	me	own	take	where
and	does	give	hold	my	pictures	the	who
animal	down	green	how	never	play	their	why
are	draw	go	I	new	pull	they	with
away	eat	goes	is	no	put	to	would
be	every	good	know	now	read	today	write
been	fall	grow	like	of	said	too	yellow
blue	far	have	little	off	see	very	you
brown	find	he	live	one	she	was	
call	for	hear	look	open	sing	water	

Decoding skills taught to date: consonants *m, s, t,* c; short *a*; consonant *n*; consonant *d*; consonant *p*; consonant *f*; short *i*; consonant *r*; consonant *h*; consonant *s* /z/; consonant *b*,; consonant *g* (hard); short *o*; consonant *l*; consonant *x*; inflection *-s*; short *e*; consonant *y*; consonant *w*; consonant *k*; consonant *v*; consonant *j*; short *u*; consonant *qu*; consonant *z*; double final consonants *ll*; double final consonants *ss*; consonants *ck*; double final consonants *ff*; double final consonants *zz*; blends with *r*; blends with *l*; blends with *s*; final blends *mp*; final blends *nt*; final blends *nd*; final blends *st*; digraph *th*; base words and ending *-s*; base words and ending *-es*; base words and ending *-ed* /ed/; base words and ending *-ed* /d/; base words and ending *-ed* /t/; base words and ending *-ing*; digraphs *ch, tch*; possessives with *'s*; digraph *sh*; digraph *wh*; digraph *ph*

The Graph Man

DECODABLE WORDS

Target Skill: **digraph *ph*** **Review digraph *th***

graph	Phil	Ralph	Ralph's	this

Previously Taught Skills

as	cans	gets	it's	plant
asked	class	his	logs	plants
bags	Club	in	man	pot
big	fill	is	on	red
black	fills	it	pens	will

SKILLS APPLIED IN WORDS IN STORY: consonants *m, s, t, c*; short *a*; consonant *n*; consonant *d*; consonant *p*; short *i*; consonant *h*; consonant *s* /z/; consonant *b*; consonant *g* (hard); short *o*; consonant *l*; inflection *-s*; short *e*; consonant *w*; double final consonants *ll*; double final consonants *ss*; consonants *ck*; blends with *r*; blends with *s*; final blend *nt*; final blend *nd*; digraph *th*; base words and ending *-s*; base words and ending *-ed* /t/; possessives with *'s*; digraph *ph*

HIGH-FREQUENCY WORDS

a	for	how	new	too
be	Green	likes	the	
blue	grows	makes	today	

Houghton Mifflin Harcourt

digraph *ph*

BOOK 96

The Graph Man

Phil gets a fish. Phil gets a bug. Steph is mad. Steph has no fish. She has no bug.

Steph tosses a rock in the pond.

Plop!

Phil swims fast. No fish. No bug. What went plop?

Steph sees bugs and fish. Steph gets them.
Phil still hunts for that plop.

Phil and Steph

Phil and Steph are ducks. They swim in the pond. They eat fish and bugs.

High-Frequency Words Taught to Date

Grade 1

a	cold	friend	help	make	our	small	we
after	come	full	her	many	out	some	what
all	do	funny	here	me	own	take	where
and	does	give	hold	my	pictures	the	who
animal	down	green	how	never	play	their	why
are	draw	go	I	new	pull	they	with
away	eat	goes	is	no	put	to	would
be	every	good	know	now	read	today	write
been	fall	grow	like	of	said	too	yellow
blue	far	have	little	off	see	very	you
brown	find	he	live	one	she	was	
call	for	hear	look	open	sing	water	

Decoding skills taught to date: consonants *m, s, t,* c ; short *a*; consonant *n*; consonant *d*; consonant *p*; consonant *f*; short *i*; consonant *r*; consonant *h*; consonant *s* /z/; consonant *b*,; consonant *g* (hard); short *o*; consonant *l*; consonant *x*; inflection *-s*; short *e*; consonant *y*; consonant *w*; consonant *k*; consonant *v*; consonant *j*; short *u*; consonant *qu*; consonant *z*; double final consonants *ll*; double final consonants *ss*; double final consonants *ff*; double final consonants *zz*; consonants *ck*; blends with *r*; blends with *l*; blends with *s*; final blends *mp*; final blends *nt*; final blends *nd*; final blends *st*; digraph *th*; base words and ending *-s*; base words and ending *-es*; base words and ending *-ed* /ed/; base words and ending *-ed* /d/; base words and ending *-ed* /t/; base words and ending *-ing*; digraphs *ch, tch*; possessives with *'s*; digraph *sh*; digraph *wh*; digraph *ph*

Phil and Steph

DECODABLE WORDS

Target Skill: **digraph *ph*** **Review digraphs *sh*, *th***

fish	Phil	Steph	that	them

Previously Taught Skills

and	gets	mad	still
bugs	has	plop	swim
ducks	in	pond	tosses
fast	is	rock	went

SKILLS APPLIED IN WORDS IN STORY: consonants *m, s, t, c*; short *a*; consonant *n*; consonant *d*; consonant *p*; consonant *f*; short *i*; consonant *r*; consonant *h*; consonant *s* /z/; consonant *b*; consonant *g* (hard); short *o*; consonant *l*; inflection *-s*; short *e*; consonant *w*; consonant *k*; short *u*; double final consonants *ll*; double final consonants *ss*; consonants *ck*; blends with *l*; blends with *s*; final blends *nd*; final blends *st*; final blends *nt*; digraph *th*; base words and ending *-s*; base words and ending *-es*; digraph *sh*; digraph *wh*; digraph *ph*

HIGH-FREQUENCY WORDS

a	for	she	to
are	no	the	what
eat	sees	they	

Houghton Mifflin Harcourt

digraph *ph*

BOOK 95

Phil and Steph

Pam got a whiff.
Whiff, whiff, whiff. Yum!
"When can we eat it?"
Pam asked.

"We can eat it when Gramp
gets here," said Dad.
"When, when, when will Gramp
get here?" asked Pam.

"I am here!" yelled Gramp.
"When, when, when can we eat?"

When, When, When?

"What is that?" asked Pam.
"It is hot and good," said Dad.

High-Frequency Words Taught to Date

Grade 1

a	cold	friend	help	make	our	small	we
after	come	full	her	many	out	some	what
all	do	funny	here	me	own	take	where
and	does	give	hold	my	pictures	the	who
animal	down	green	how	never	play	their	why
are	draw	go	I	new	pull	they	with
away	eat	goes	is	no	put	to	would
be	every	good	know	now	read	today	write
been	fall	grow	like	of	said	too	yellow
blue	far	have	little	off	see	very	you
brown	find	he	live	one	she	was	
call	for	hear	look	open	sing	water	

Decoding skills taught to date: consonants *m, s, t, c*; short *a*; consonant *n*; consonant *d*; consonant *p*; consonant *f*; short *i*; consonant *r*; consonant *h*; consonant *s* /z/; consonant *b*; consonant *g* (hard); short *o*; consonant *l*; consonant *x*; inflection *-s*; short *e*; consonant *y*; consonant *w*; consonant *k*; consonant *v*; consonant *j*; short *u*; consonant *qu*; consonant *z*; double final consonants *ll*; double final consonants *ss*; double final consonants *ff*; double final consonants *zz*; consonants *ck*; blends with *r*; blends with *l*; blends with *s*; final blends *mp*; final blends *nt*; final blends *nd*; final blends *st*; digraph *th*; base words and ending *-s*; base words and ending *-es*; base words and ending *-ed* /ed/; base words and ending *-ed* /d/; base words and ending *-ed* /t/; base words and ending *-ing*; digraphs *ch, tch*; possessives with *'s*; digraph *sh*; digraph *wh*

When, When, When?

DECODABLE WORDS

Target Skill: **digraph *wh***

when whiff

Previously Taught Skills

am	Dad	has	Pam	yum
and	gets	hot	that	
asked	got	is	will	
can	Gramp	it	yelled	

SKILLS APPLIED IN WORDS IN STORY: consonants *m, s, t, c*; short *a*; consonant *n*; consonant *d*; consonant *p*; consonant *f*; short *i*; consonant *r*; consonant *h*; consonant *s* /z/; consonant *g* (hard); short *o*; consonant *l*; inflection *-s*; short *e*; consonant *y*; consonant *w*; short *u*; double final consonants *ll*; double final consonants *ff*; blends with *r*; blends with *l*; blends with *s*; final blend *mp*; final blend *nd*; digraph *th*; digraph *wh*

HIGH-FREQUENCY WORDS

a	good	I	we
eat	here	said	**wh**at

Houghton Mifflin Harcourt

digraph *wh*

BOOK 94

When, When, When?

Bob whips, whips, whips the mix. The mix puffs up. It looks like fluff!

Jill gets a whiff. Yum!
"When can we eat?" asks Jill.
"When, when, when?"

Bob gets cups for them. Bob puts the fluff mix in two cups. The fluff is big in one cup. Which cup will Jill pick?

Whip the Mix

Bob has a whisk. Bob can whip the mix with his whisk.

High-Frequency Words Taught to Date

Grade 1

a
after
all
and
animal
are
away
be
been
blue
brown
call
cold
come
do
does
down
draw
eat
every
fall
far
find
for
friend
full
funny
give
green
go
goes
good
grow
have
he
hear
help
her
here
hold
how
I
is
know
like
little
live
look
make
many
me
my
never
new
no
now
of
off
one
open
our
out
own
pictures
play
pull
put
read
said
see
she
sing
small
some
take
their
the
they
to
today
too
very
was
water
we
what
where
who
why
with
would
write
yellow
you

Decoding skills taught to date: consonants *m, s, t,* c; short *a*; consonant *n*; consonant *d*; consonant *p*; consonant *f*; short *i*; consonant *r*; consonant *h*; consonant *s* /z/; consonant *b*; consonant *g* (hard); short *o*; consonant *l*; consonant *x*, inflection *–s*; short *e*; consonant *y*; consonant *w*; consonant *k*; consonant *v*; consonant *j*; short *u*; consonant *qu*; consonant *z*; double final consonants *ll*; double final consonants *ss*; consonants *-ck*; double final consonants *ff*; double final consonants *zz*; blends with *r*; blends with *l*; blends with *s*; final blend *mp*; final blend *nt*; final blend *nd*; final blend *st*; digraph *th*; base words and ending *–s*; base words and ending *–es*; base words and ending *–ed* /ed/; base words and ending *–ed* /d/; base words and ending *–ed* /t/; base words and ending *–ing*; digraphs *ch, tch*; possessives with *'s*; digraph *sh*; digraph *wh*

Whip the Mix

DECODABLE WORDS

Target Skill: **digraph *wh***

when	whiff	whips
which	whip	whisk

Previously Taught Skills

asks	fluff	is	puffs	yum
big	gets	it	them	
Bob	has	Jill	up	
can	his	mix	will	
cups	in	pick	with	

SKILLS APPLIED IN WORDS IN STORY: consonants *m, s, t, c*; short *a*; consonant *n*; consonant *p*; consonant *f*; short *i*; consonant *h*; consonant *s* /z/; consonant *b*; consonant *g* (hard); short *o*; consonant *x*, inflection –*s*; short *e*; consonant *y*; consonant *w*; consonant *j*; short *u*; double final consonants *ll*; consonants *ck*; double final consonants *ff*; blends with *l*; blends with *s*; digraph *th*; base words and ending –*s*; digraph *wh*

HIGH-FREQUENCY WORDS

a	for	looks	one	two
eat	like	puts	the	we

Houghton Mifflin Harcourt

digraph *wh*

BOOK 93

Whip the Mix

Shell sells snacks.

Shell sells fresh fish sticks.

Shell shuts the ship shop.
Shell tells her friend he can
come back if it is open.

Ship Shop

Shell has a ship shop.

High-Frequency Words Taught to Date

Grade 1

a
after
all
and
animal
are
away
be
been
blue
brown
call
cold
come
do
does
down
draw
eat
every
fall
far
find
for
friend
full
funny
give
go
goes
good
green
grow
have
he
hear
help
her
here
hold
how
I
is
know
like
little
live
look
make
many
me
my
never
new
no
now
of
off
one
open
our
out
own
pictures
play
pull
put
read
said
see
she
sing
small
some
take
the
their
they
to
today
too
very
was
water
we
what
where
who
why
with
would
write
yellow
you

Decoding skills taught to date: consonants *m, s, t,* c; short *a*; consonant *n*; consonant *d*; consonant *p*; consonant *f*; short *i*; consonant *r*; consonant *h*; consonant *s* /z/; consonant *b*; consonant *g* (hard); short *o*; consonant *l*; consonant *x*, inflection *-s*; short *e*; consonant *y*; consonant *w*; consonant *k*; consonant *v*; consonant *j*; short *u*; consonant *qu*; consonant *z*; double final consonants *ll*; double final consonants *ss*; double final consonants *ff*; double final consonants *zz*; consonants *-ck*; blends with *r*; blends with *l*; blends with *s*; final blend *mp*; final blend *nt*; final blend *nd*; final blend *st*; digraph *th*; base words and ending *-s*; base words and ending *-es*; base words and ending *-ed* /ed/; base words and ending *-ed* /d/; base words and ending *-ed* /t/; base words and ending *-ing*; digraphs *ch, tch*; possessives with *'s*; digraph *sh*

Ship Shop

DECODABLE WORDS

Target Skill: **digraph *sh***

fish	Shell	shop
fresh	ship	shuts

Previously Taught Skills

back	has	is	sells	sticks
can	if	it	snacks	tells

SKILLS APPLIED IN WORDS IN STORY: consonants *s, c, t*; short *a*; consonant *n*; consonant *p*; consonant *f*; short *i*; consonant *r*; consonant *h*; consonant *s* /z/; consonant *b*; inflection -*s*; short *e*; consonant *k*; double final consonants *ll*; consonants *ck*; blends with *r*; blends with *s*

HIGH-FREQUENCY WORDS

a	friend	her	the
come	he	open	to

Houghton Mifflin Harcourt

Ship Shop

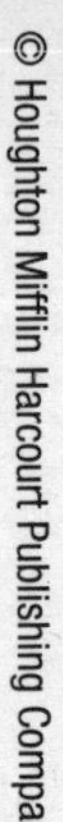

Shag goes in a tub.
Shag gets wet.
Splish, splash! Splish, splash!

I brush Shag.
Brush, brush, brush, brush.

Shag does not shed.
Shag looks fresh and new.

Shag Sheds

Shag sheds.
Shag sheds a lot.

High-Frequency Words Taught to Date

Grade 1

a	cold	friend	help	make	our	small	we
after	come	full	her	many	out	some	what
all	do	funny	here	me	own	take	where
and	does	give	hold	my	pictures	the	who
animal	down	go	how	never	play	their	why
are	draw	goes	I	new	pull	they	with
away	eat	good	is	no	put	to	would
be	every	green	know	now	read	today	write
been	fall	grow	like	of	said	too	yellow
blue	far	have	little	off	see	very	you
brown	find	he	live	one	she	was	
call	for	hear	look	open	sing	water	

Decoding skills taught to date: consonants *m, s, t, c,* short *a*; consonant *n*; consonant *d*; consonant *p*; consonant *f*; short *i*; consonant *r*; consonant *h*; consonant *s /z/*; consonant *b*; hard *g*; short *o*; consonant *l*; consonant *x*; inflection *s*; short *e*; consonant *y*; consonant *w*; consonant *k*; consonant *v*; consonant *j*; short *u*; consonants *qu*; consonant *z*; double final consonants *ll*; double final consonants *ss*; consonants *ck*, double final consonants *ff*; double final consonants *zz*; blends with *r*; blends with *l*; blends with *s*; final blends *mp*; final blends *nt*; final blends *nd*; final blends *st*; digraph *th*; base words and ending *–s*; base words and ending *–es*; base words and ending *–ed /ed/*; base words and ending *–ed /d/*; base words and ending *–ed /t/*; base words and ending *–ing*; digraphs *ch, tch*; possessive with *'s*; digraph *sh*

Shag Sheds

DECODABLE WORDS

Target Skill: **digraph *sh***

brush	Shag	sheds	splish
fresh	shed	splash	

Previously Taught Skills

and	goes	lot	tub
gets	in	not	wet

SKILLS APPLIED IN WORDS IN STORY: consonants *s, t,* short *a*; consonant *n*; consonant *d*; consonant *p*; consonant *f*; short *i*; consonant *r*; consonant *h*; consonant *s* /z/; consonant *b*; hard *g*; short *o*; consonant *l*; inflection *s*; short *e*; consonant *w*; short *u*; blends with *r*; blends with *l*; blends with *s*; final blends *nd*; base words and ending *–s*; digraph *sh*

HIGH-FREQUENCY WORDS

a	does	I	looks	new

Houghton Mifflin Harcourt.

digraph *sh*

BOOK 91

Shag Sheds

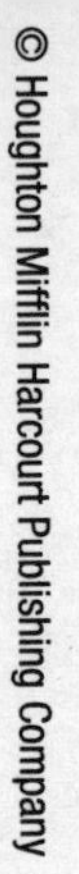

Jen, Sam, and Liz had to go.
Bill's mom got their hats.
She picked up the red hat.
"That is Jen's hat," said Bill.
Jen had her hat.

Mom picked up the black hat.
"That is Sam's hat," said Bill.
Sam had his hat.
Mom picked up the blue hat.
"That is Liz's hat," said Bill.
Liz had her hat.

Mom picked up the brown hat.
"That is not a hat!" yelled Liz.
"It is Bill's pet cat, Jack!"

A Stack of Hats

Jen, Sam, and Liz went to Bill's.
They set their hats in a stack.

High-Frequency Words Taught to Date

Grade 1

a	call	friend	here	many	own	some	we
after	cold	full	hold	me	pictures	take	what
all	come	funny	how	my	play	the	where
and	do	give	I	never	pull	their	who
animal	does	go	is	no	put	they	why
are	draw	good	know	now	read	to	with
away	eat	have	like	of	said	today	would
be	every	he	little	off	see	too	write
been	far	hear	live	one	she	very	you
blue	find	help	look	our	sing	was	
brown	for	her	make	out	small	water	

Decoding skills taught to date: consonants *m, s, t, c*; short *a*; consonant *n*; consonant *d*; consonant *p*; consonant *f*; short *i*; consonant *r*; consonant *h*; /z/ spelled *s*; consonant *b*; consonant *g* (hard); short *o*; consonant *l*; consonant *x*; inflection *-s*; short *e*; consonant *y*; consonant *w*; consonant *k*; consonant *v*; consonant *j*; short *u*; /kw/ spelled *qu*; consonant *z*; final consonants *ll*; final consonants *ss*; consonants *ck*; final consonants *ff*; final consonants *zz*; blends with *r*; blends with *l*; blends with *s*; final blend *mp*; final blend *nt*; final blend *nd*; final blend *st*; digraph *th*; ending *-s*; ending *-es*; ending *-ed* /ĕd/; ending *-ed* /d/; ending *-ed* /t/; ending *-ing*; digraphs *ch, tch*; possessives with *'s*

A Stack of Hats

DECODABLE WORDS

Target Skill: **possessives with *'s***

Bill's	Jen's	Liz's	Sam's

Previously Taught Skills

and	hat	Jen	red	went
Bill	hats	Liz	Sam	yelled
black	in	mom	set	
cat	is	not	stack	
got	it	pet	that	

SKILLS APPLIED IN WORDS IN STORY: consonants *m, s, c, t*; short *a*; consonant *n*; consonant *d*; consonant *p*; short *i*; consonant *r*; consonant *h*; /z/ spelled *s*; consonant *b*; consonant *g* (hard); short *o*; consonant *l*; short *e*; consonant *y*; consonant *w*; consonant *j*; short *u*; consonant *z*; final consonants *ll*; consonants *-ck*; blends with *l*; blends with *s*; final blend *nt*; final blend *nd*; digraph *th*; ending *-s*; ending *-ed* /d/; ending *-ed* /t/; possessives with *'s*

HIGH-FREQUENCY WORDS

a	her	the
blue	of	their
brown	said	they
go	she	to

Houghton Mifflin Harcourt

possessives with *'s*

BOOK 90

A Stack of Hats

Bob's friend Tom has a pet dog.
Tom's dog is Buck.

Bob's mom and dad see Bob with Buck.
They said, "Bob is good with this dog. We **can** get a pet for Bob."

Bob's mom and dad get Bob a pup. Bob's pup is Spot! Now Bob has a pet.

Bob's Pet

Bob has no pet. Bob's mom has a pet cat. Bob's sis has a pet rat. Bob's dad has a pet frog.

High-Frequency Words Taught to Date

Grade 1

a	call	friend	here	many	own	some	we
after	cold	full	hold	me	pictures	take	what
all	come	funny	how	my	play	the	where
and	do	give	I	never	pull	their	who
animal	does	go	is	no	put	they	why
are	draw	good	know	now	read	to	with
away	eat	have	like	of	said	today	would
be	every	he	little	off	see	too	write
been	far	hear	live	one	she	very	you
blue	find	help	look	our	sing	was	
brown	for	her	make	out	small	water	

Decoding skills taught to date: consonants *m, s, c, t*; short *a*; consonant *n*; consonant *d*; consonant *p*; consonant *f*; short *i*; consonant *r*; consonant *h*; /z/ spelled *s*; consonant *b*; consonant *g* (hard); short *o*; consonant *l*; consonant *x*; inflection *-s*; short *e*; consonant *y*; consonant *w*; consonant *k*; consonant *v*; consonant *j*; short *u*; /kw/ spelled *qu*; consonant *z*; final consonants *ll*; final consonants *ss*; consonants *-ck*; final consonants *ff*; final consonants *zz*; blends with *r*; blends with *l*; blends with *s*; final blend *mp*; final blend *nt*; final blend *nd*; final blend *st*; digraph *th*; ending *-s*; ending *-es*; ending *-ed* /ĕd/; ending *-ed* /d/; ending *-ed* /t/; ending *-ing*; digraphs *ch, tch*; possessives with *'s*

Bob's Pet

DECODABLE WORDS

Target Skill: possessives with *'s*

Bob's Tom's

Previously Taught Skills

and	dog	mom	Spot
Bob	frog	pet	this
Buck	get	pets	Tom
can	has	pup	with
cat	his	rat	
dad	is	sis	

SKILLS APPLIED IN WORDS IN STORY: consonants *m, s, c, t*; short *a*; consonant *n*; consonant *d*; consonant *p*; short *i*; consonant *r*; consonant *h*; /z/ spelled *s*; consonant *b*; consonant *g* (hard); short *o*; short *e*; short *u*; consonants *-ck*; blends with *r*; blends with *s*; final blend *nd*; possessives with *'s*

HIGH-FREQUENCY WORDS

a	good	said	we
for	no	see	
friend	now	they	

Houghton Mifflin Harcourt

possessives with *'s*

BOOK 89

Bob's Pet

Chip has a black patch on his back. Kitch has a black patch on his back, too.

Chip and Kitch will chomp on this.

The hutch has a latch. Chip and Kitch will not get out. Chip and Kitch can nap.

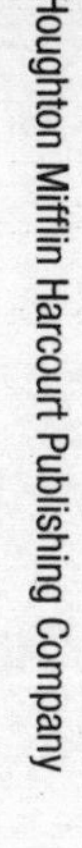

Chip and Kitch

I have two pets, Chip and Kitch. Chip and Kitch live in a hutch.

High-Frequency Words Taught to Date

Grade 1

a	come	go	like	one	small	what
after	do	good	little	our	some	where
all	does	have	live	out	take	who
and	draw	he	look	own	the	why
animal	eat	hear	make	pictures	their	with
are	every	help	many	play	they	would
away	far	her	me	pull	to	write
be	find	here	my	put	today	you
been	for	hold	never	read	too	
blue	friend	how	no	said	very	
brown	full	I	now	see	was	
call	funny	is	of	she	water	
cold	give	know	off	sing	we	

Decoding skills taught to date: consonants *m, s, t,* c; short *a*; consonant *n*; consonant *d*; consonant *p*; consonant *f*; short *i*; consonant *r*; consonant *h*; /z/ spelled *s*; consonant *b*; consonant *g* (hard); short *o*; consonant *l*; consonant *x*, inflection *-s*; short *e*; consonant *y*; consonant *w*; consonant *k*; consonant *v*; consonant *j*; short *u*; /kw/ spelled *qu*; consonant *z*; final consonants *ll*; final consonants *ss*; consonants *-ck*; final consonants *ff*; final consonants *zz*; blends with *r*; blends with *l*; blends with *s*; final blend *mp*; final blend *nt*; final blend *nd*; final blend *st*; digraph *th*; ending *-s*; ending *-es*; ending *-ed* /ĕd/; ending *-ed* /d/; ending *-ed* /t/; ending *-ing*; digraphs *ch, tch*

Chip and Kitch

DECODABLE WORDS

Target Skill: **digraphs *ch*, *tch***

Chip	hutch	latch
chomp	Kitch	patch

Previously Taught Skills

and	can	his	not	this
back	get	in	on	will
black	has	nap	pets	

SKILLS APPLIED IN WORDS IN STORY: consonants *s, t, c*; short *a*; consonant *n*; consonant *d;* consonant *p*; short *i*; consonant *h*; /z/ spelled *s*; consonant *b*; consonant *g* (hard); short *o*; consonant *l*; inflection *-s*; short *e*; consonant *w*; consonant *k*; short *u*; final consonants *ll*; consonants *ck*; blends with *l*; final blend *mp*; final blend *nd*; digraph *th*; ending *-s*; digraphs *ch, tch*

HIGH-FREQUENCY WORDS

a	I	out	too
have	live	the	two

Houghton Mifflin Harcourt

digraphs *ch*, *tch*

BOOK 88

Chip and Kitch

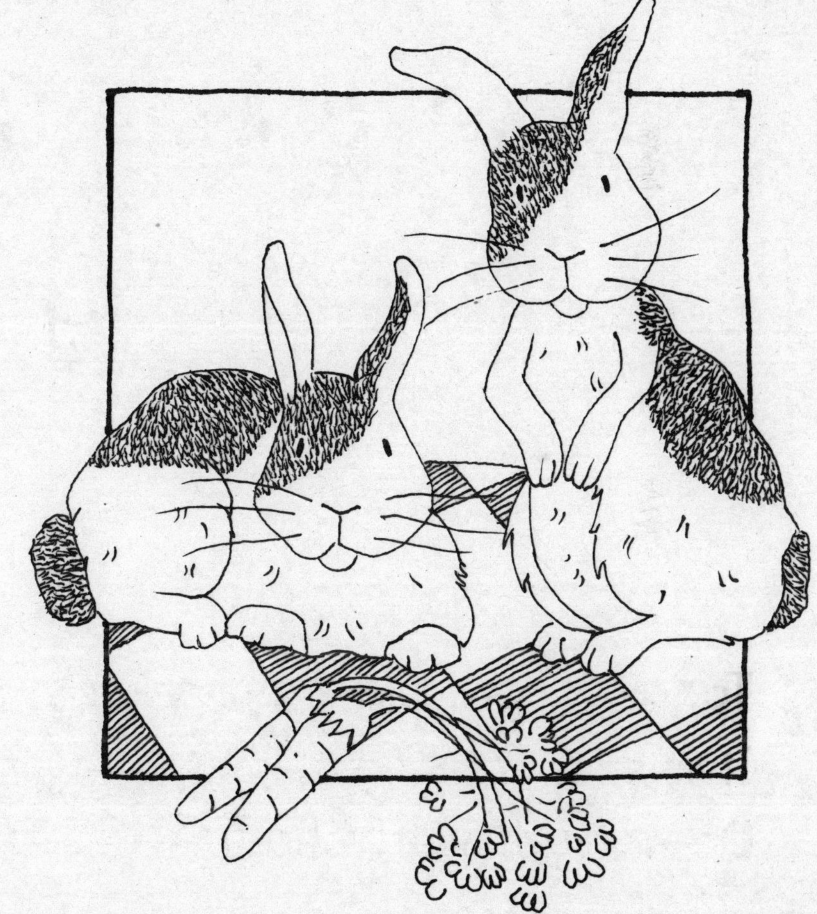

Today, Chad and Dutch play.
It is such fun!
Do not get wet, Chad!

It gets cold.
Chad and Dutch get a chill.
They run away from the wind.

Then Chad and Dutch fetch some chips.

Chad and Dutch

Chad and Dutch are pals. Chad and Dutch chat after class.

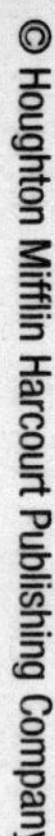

High-Frequency Words Taught to Date

Grade 1

a	come	go	like	one	small	what
after	do	good	little	our	some	where
all	does	have	live	out	take	who
and	draw	he	look	own	the	why
animal	eat	hear	make	pictures	their	with
are	every	help	many	play	they	would
away	far	her	me	pull	to	write
be	find	here	my	put	today	you
been	for	hold	never	read	too	
blue	friend	how	no	said	very	
brown	full	I	now	see	was	
call	funny	is	of	she	water	
cold	give	know	off	sing	we	

Decoding skills taught to date: consonants *m, s, t,* c; short *a*; consonant *n*; consonant *d*; consonant *p*; consonant *f*; short *i*; consonant *r*; consonant *h*; /z/ spelled *s*; consonant *b*; consonant *g* (hard); short *o*; consonant *l*; consonant *x*, inflection *-s*; short *e*; consonant *y*; consonant *w*; consonant *k*; consonant *v*; consonant *j*; short *u*; /kw/ spelled *qu*; consonant *z*; final consonants *ll*; final consonants *ss*; consonants *-ck*; final consonants *ff*; final consonants *zz*; blends with *r*; blends with *l*; blends with *s*; final blend *mp*; final blend *nt*; final blend *nd*; final blend *st*; digraph *th*; ending *-s*; ending *-es*; ending *-ed* /ĕd/; ending *-ed* /d/; ending *-ed* /t/; ending *-ing*; digraphs *ch, tch*

Chad and Dutch

DECODABLE WORDS

Target Skill: **digraphs *ch*, *tch***

Chad	chill	Dutch	such
chat	chips	fetch	

Previously Taught Skills

and	get	not	wet
class	gets	pals	wind
fun	is	run	
from	it	then	

SKILLS APPLIED IN WORDS IN STORY: consonants *m, s, t, c*; short *a*; consonant *n*; consonant *d;* consonant *p*; consonant *f*; short *i*; consonant *r*; /z/ spelled *s*; consonant *g* (hard); short *o*; consonant *l*; inflection *-s*; short *e*; consonant *w*; short *u*; final consonants *ll*; final consonants *ss*; blends with *r*; blends with *l*; final blend *nd*; digraph *th*; ending *-s*; digraphs *ch, tch*

HIGH-FREQUENCY WORDS

a	away	play	they
after	cold	some	today
are	do	the	

Houghton Mifflin Harcourt

digraphs *ch*, *tch*

BOOK 87

Chad and Dutch

Hal is looking at the van.
He is pulling on this and that.
He is fixing it.
That is his job.

It is fixed.
Now Hal is waxing and buffing the van.
Hal will make it look good!

Hal is filling the van with gas.
Then this van will be set to go!

Hal Is Doing His Job

Hal fixes stuff.
This van will not go.
Hal is pulling it with his truck.
He will fix it.

High-Frequency Words Taught to Date

Grade 1

a	cold	friend	her	make	play	take	what
after	come	full	here	many	pull	the	where
all	do	funny	hold	me	put	their	who
and	does	give	how	my	read	they	why
animal	draw	go	I	no	said	to	with
are	eat	good	is	now	see	today	would
away	every	have	like	of	she	too	write
be	far	he	little	one	sing	was	you
blue	find	hear	live	our	small	water	
call	for	help	look	pictures	some	we	

Decoding skills taught to date: consonants *m, s, t,* c; short *a*; consonant *n*; consonant *d*; consonant *p*; consonant *f*; short *i*; consonant *r*; consonant *h*; /z/ spelled *s*; consonant *b*; consonant *g* (hard); short *o*; consonant *l*; consonant *x*, inflection *-s*; short *e*; consonant *y*; consonant *w*; consonant *k*; consonant *v*; consonant *j*; short *u*; /kw/ spelled *qu*; consonant *z*; final consonants *ll*; final consonants *ss*; consonants *ck*; final consonants *ff*; final consonants *zz*; blends with *r*; blends with *l*; blends with *s*; final blend *mp*; final blend *nt*; final blend *nd*; final blend *st*; digraph *th*; ending *-s*; ending *-es*; ending *-ed* /ĕd/; ending *-ed* /d/; ending *-ed* /t/; ending *-ing*

Hal Is Doing His Job

DECODABLE WORDS

Target Skill: **ending *-ing***

buffing	fixing
filling	waxing

Previously Taught Skills

and	gas	job	then	with
at	Hal	not	this	
fix	his	on	truck	
fixed	is	stuff	van	
fixes	it	that	will	

SKILLS APPLIED IN WORDS IN STORY: consonants *s, t*; short *a*; consonant *n*; consonant *f*; short *i*; consonant *r;* consonant *h*; /z/ spelled *s*; consonant *b*; consonant *g* (hard); short *o*; consonant *l*; consonant *x*; consonant *w*; consonant *v*; consonant *j*; short *u*; final consonants *ll*; consonants *ck*; final consonants *ff*; digraph *th*; blends with *r*; blends with *s*; final blend *nd*; ending *-es*; ending *-ed* /t/; ending *-ing*

HIGH-FREQUENCY WORDS

do(ing)	he	make	the
go	look	now	
good	look(ing)	pull(ing)	

Houghton Mifflin Harcourt

ending *-ing*

BOOK 86

Hal Is Doing His Job

Now Val is looking up.
But Puff is not going to jump yet.

At last, Puff is jumping.
He will be glad to get to Val.

Val is rocking Puff.
Puff is licking Val.

Is Puff Missing?

Val is calling her cat Puff.
Val does not look up.
She does not spot Puff.
But Puff spots Val!

High-Frequency Words Taught to Date

Grade 1

a	cold	friend	her	make	play	take	what
after	come	full	here	many	pull	the	where
all	do	funny	hold	me	put	their	who
and	does	give	how	my	read	they	why
animal	draw	go	I	no	said	to	with
are	eat	good	is	now	see	today	would
away	every	have	like	of	she	too	write
be	far	he	little	one	sing	was	you
blue	find	hear	live	our	small	water	
call	for	help	look	pictures	some	we	

Decoding skills taught to date: consonants *m, s, t,* c; short *a*; consonant *n*; consonant *d*; consonant *p*; consonant *f*, short *i*; consonant *r*; consonant *h*; /z/ spelled *s*; consonant *b*; consonant *g* (hard); short *o*; consonant *l*; consonant *x*, inflection *-s*; short *e*; consonant *y*; consonant *w*; consonant *k*; consonant *v*; consonant *j*; short *u*; /kw/ spelled *qu*; consonant *z*; final consonants *ll*; final consonants *ss*; consonants *ck*; final consonants *ff*; final consonants *zz*; blends with *r*; blends with *l*; blends with *s*; final blend *mp*; final blend *nt*; final blend *nd*; final blend *st*; digraph *th*; ending *-s*; ending *-es*; ending *-ed* /ĕd/; ending *-ed* /d/; ending *-ed* /t/; ending *-ing*

Is Puff Missing?

DECODABLE WORDS

Target Skill: **ending *-ing***

calling	licking	missing
jumping	looking	rocking

Previously Taught Skills

at	glad	Puff	Val
but	is	spot	will
cat	last	spots	yet
get	not	up	

SKILLS APPLIED IN WORDS IN STORY: consonants *m, s, c, t*; short *a*; consonant *n*; consonant *d*; consonant *p*; short *i*; consonant *r*; /z/ spelled *s*; consonant *b*; consonant *g* (hard); short *o*; consonant *l*; inflection *-s*; short *e*; consonant *y*; consonant *w*; consonant *v*; consonant *j*; short *u*; final consonants *ss*; consonants *ck*; final consonants *ll*; final consonants *ff*; blends with *l*; blends with *s*; final blend *mp*; final blend *st*; ending *-ing*

HIGH-FREQUENCY WORDS

be	he	now	to
does	her	see(s)	
go(ing)	look	she	

Houghton Mifflin Harcourt

ending *-ing*

BOOK 85

Is Puff Missing?

The pigs locked the hut.
Max kicked, and the hut rocked.
But Max did not get in.

Max went up to jump in.
He jumped! He missed!

Max landed with a plop.
Go away, Max.

Will Max Get In?

Max said, "Let me in, pigs!"
But the pigs did not let Max in.
Max huffed and puffed.
But the hut just bent.

High-Frequency Words Taught to Date

Grade 1

a	cold	friend	her	make	play	take	what
after	come	full	here	many	pull	the	where
all	do	funny	hold	me	put	their	who
and	does	give	how	my	read	they	why
animal	draw	go	I	no	said	to	with
are	eat	good	is	now	see	today	would
away	every	have	like	of	she	too	write
be	far	he	little	one	sing	was	you
blue	find	hear	live	our	small	water	
call	for	help	look	pictures	some	we	

Decoding skills taught to date: consonants *m, s, t,* c; short *a*; consonant *n*; consonant *d*; consonant *p*; consonant *f*; short *i*; consonant *r*; consonant *h*; /z/ spelled *s*; consonant *b*; consonant *g* (hard); short *o*; consonant *l*; consonant *x*, inflection *-s*; short *e*; consonant *y*; consonant *w*; consonant *k*; consonant *v*; consonant *j*; short *u*; /kw/ spelled *qu*; consonant *z*; final consonants *ll*; final consonants *ss*; consonants *ck*; final consonants *ff*; final consonants *zz*; blends with *r*; blends with *l*; blends with *s*; final blend *mp*; final blend *nt*; final blend *nd*; final blend *st*; digraph *th*; ending *-s*; ending *-es*; ending *-ed* /ĕd/; ending *-ed* /d/; ending *-ed* /t/

Will Max Get In?

DECODABLE WORDS

Target Skill: **ending *-ed* /t/**

huffed	kicked	missed	rocked
jumped	locked	puffed	

Previously Taught Skills

and	get	just	not	went
bent	hut	landed	pigs	will
but	in	let	plop	with
did	jump	Max	up	

SKILLS APPLIED IN WORDS IN STORY: consonants *m, s, t;* short *a*; consonant *n*; consonant *d*; consonant *p*; short *i*; consonant *r*; consonant *h*; consonant *b*; consonant *g* (hard); short *o*; consonant *l*; consonant *x*; short *e*; consonant *w*; consonant *k*; consonant *j*; short *u*; final consonants *ss*; consonants *ck*; final consonants *ff*; final consonants *ll*; blends with *l*; final blend *nd*; final blend *nt*; final blend *st*; digraph *th*; ending *-s*; ending *-ed* /ĕd/; ending *-ed* /t/

HIGH-FREQUENCY WORDS

a	go	me	the
away	he	said	to

Houghton Mifflin Harcourt

Will Max Get In?

Then the ducks quacked at Bev.
Bev looked at them.
Bev asked them, "Can you eat
what is in this bag?"
The ducks just quacked.

Bev tossed the ducks a snack.
They pecked at it.

The ducks did like that snack!
Bev ran on to tell her dad.

Ducks Snack

Bev passed ducks in their pen.
They did not quack.
Bev did not see them.

High-Frequency Words Taught to Date

Grade 1

a	cold	friend	her	make	play	take	what
after	come	full	here	many	pull	the	where
all	do	funny	hold	me	put	their	who
and	does	give	how	my	read	they	why
animal	draw	go	I	no	said	to	with
are	eat	good	is	now	see	today	would
away	every	have	like	of	she	too	write
be	far	he	little	one	sing	was	you
blue	find	hear	live	our	small	water	
call	for	help	look	pictures	some	we	

Decoding skills taught to date: consonants *m, s, t,* c; short *a*; consonant *n*; consonant *d*; consonant *p*; consonant *f*; short *i*; consonant *r*; consonant *h*; /z/ spelled *s*; consonant *b*; consonant *g* (hard); short *o*; consonant *l*; consonant *x*, inflection *-s*; short *e*; consonant *y*; consonant *w*; consonant *k*; consonant *v*; consonant *j*; short *u*; /kw/ spelled *qu*; consonant *z*; final consonants *ll*; final consonants *ss*; consonants *ck*; final consonants *ff*; final consonants *zz*; blends with *r*; blends with *l*; blends with *s*; final blend *mp*; final blend *nt*; final blend *nd*; final blend *st*; digraph *th*; ending *-s*; ending *-es*; ending *-ed* /ĕd/; ending *-ed* /d/; ending *-ed* /t/

Ducks Snack

DECODABLE WORDS

Target Skill: ending *-ed* /t/

asked	passed	pecked	quacked	tossed

Previously Taught Skills

at	did	just	ran	then
bag	ducks	not	snack	this
Bev	in	on	tell	
can	is	pen	that	
dad	it	quack	them	

SKILLS APPLIED IN WORDS IN STORY: consonants *m, s, c, t;* short *a*; consonant *n*; consonant *d*; consonant *p*; short *i*; consonant *r*; /z/ spelled *s*; consonant *b*; consonant *g* (hard); short *o*; inflection *-s*; short *e*; consonant *k*; consonant *v*; consonant *j*; short *u*; /kw/ spelled *qu*; final consonants *ll*; final consonants *ss*; consonants *ck*; blends with *s*; final blend *st*; digraph *th*; ending *-s*; ending *-ed* /t/

HIGH-FREQUENCY WORDS

a	like	the	to
eat	look(ed)	their	what
her	see	they	you

Houghton Mifflin Harcourt

ending *-ed* /t/

BOOK 83

Ducks Snack

Cliff spilled sand from the pot and put sand in a can. What did Rex do? Rex just sat.

Cliff added six cans of sand. "Look at that, Rex!" Cliff said. What did Rex do then?

"No, Rex!" yelled Cliff.
But Rex just sat.

ending -*ed* /d/

BOOK 82

Cliff and Rex

Cliff filled a big pot with sand.
What did Rex do?
Rex just sat.

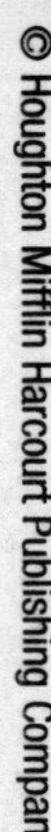

High-Frequency Words Taught to Date

Grade 1

a	cold	friend	her	make	play	take	what
after	come	full	here	many	pull	the	where
all	do	funny	hold	me	put	their	who
and	does	give	how	my	read	they	why
animal	draw	go	I	no	said	to	with
are	eat	good	is	now	see	today	would
away	every	have	like	of	she	too	write
be	far	he	little	one	sing	was	you
blue	find	hear	live	our	small	water	
call	for	help	look	pictures	some	we	

Decoding skills taught to date: consonants *m, s, t,* c; short *a*; consonant *n*; consonant *d*; consonant *p*; consonant *f*; short *i*; consonant *r*; consonant *h*; /z/ spelled *s*; consonant *b*; consonant *g* (hard); short *o*; consonant *l*; consonant *x*, inflection *-s*; short *e*; consonant *y*; consonant *w*; consonant *k*; consonant *v*; consonant *j*; short *u*; /kw/ spelled *qu*; consonant *z*; final consonants *ll*; final consonants *ss*; consonants *ck*; final consonants *ff*; final consonants *zz*; blends with *r*; blends with *l*; blends with *s*; final blend *mp*; final blend *nt*; final blend *nd*; final blend *st*; digraph *th*; ending *-s*; ending *-es*; ending *-ed* /ĕd/; ending *-ed* /d/

Cliff and Rex

DECODABLE WORDS

Target Skill: **ending *-ed* /d/**

added	filled	spilled	yelled

Previously Taught Skills

and	can	from	Rex	that
at	cans	in	sand	then
big	Cliff	just	sat	with
but	did	pot	six	

SKILLS APPLIED IN WORDS IN STORY: consonants *m, s, c, t*; short *a*; consonant *n*; consonant *d*; consonant *p*; consonant *f*; short *i*; consonant *r*; consonant *b*; consonant *g* (hard); short *o*; consonant *l*; consonant *x*; short *e*; consonant *y*; consonant *w*; consonant *j*; short *u*; final consonants *ll*; final consonants *ff*; blends with *r*; blends with *l*; blends with *s*; final blend *nd*; final blend *st*; digraph *th*; ending *-s*; ending *-ed* /ĕd/; ending *-ed* /d/

HIGH-FREQUENCY WORDS

a	no	said	what
do	of	the	
look	put	to	

Houghton Mifflin Harcourt

ending *-ed* /d/

BOOK 82

Cliff and Rex

Then Jon and Tam went past
Stef.
Stef had a stand.
Tam wanted to stop at the stand.

Jon filled a cup and handed it
to his sis.
Stef said, "That will help.
Now Tam will not yell."

Jon went to pull his sis.
Tam did not make it fun!
Tam yelled!

Tam Yelled

Jon pulled his sis on the path.
Tam did not make it fun.
Tam yelled.

High-Frequency Words Taught to Date

Grade 1

a	cold	friend	her	make	play	take	what
after	come	full	here	many	pull	the	where
all	do	funny	hold	me	put	their	who
and	does	give	how	my	read	they	why
animal	draw	go	I	no	said	to	with
are	eat	good	is	now	see	today	would
away	every	have	like	of	she	too	write
be	far	he	little	one	sing	was	you
blue	find	hear	live	our	small	water	
call	for	help	look	pictures	some	we	

Decoding skills taught to date: consonants *m, s, t,* c; short *a*; consonant *n*; consonant *d*; consonant *p*; consonant *f*; short *i*; consonant *r*; consonant *h*; /z/ spelled *s*; consonant *b*; consonant *g* (hard); short *o*; consonant *l*; consonant *x*; inflection *-s*; short *e*; consonant *y*; consonant *w*; consonant *k*; consonant *v*; consonant *j*; short *u*; /kw/ spelled *qu*; consonant *z*; final consonants *ll*; final consonants *ss*; final consonants *ff*; final consonants *zz*; consonants *ck*; blends with *r*; blends with *l*; blends with *s*; final blend *mp*; final blend *nt*; final blend *nd*; final blend *st*; digraph *th*; base words and ending *-s*; ending *-es*; ending *-ed* /ĕd/; ending *-ed* /d/

Tam Yelled

DECODABLE WORDS

Target Skill: **ending *-ed* /d/**

filled	pulled	yelled		

Previously Taught Skills

and	handed	on	stop	with
at	help	past	Tam	yell
cup	his	path	that	
did	it	sis	then	
fun	Jon	stand	went	
had	not	Stef	will	

SKILLS APPLIED IN WORDS IN STORY: consonants *m, s, t, c*; short *a*; consonant *n*; consonant *d*; consonant *p*; consonant *f*; short *i*; consonant *h*; /z/ spelled *s*; short *o*; consonant *l*; short *e*; consonant *y*; consonant *w*; consonant *j*; short *u*; final consonants *ll*; blends with *s*; final blend *nt*; final blend *nd*; final blend *st*; digraph *th*; ending /ĕd/; ending *-ed* /d/

HIGH-FREQUENCY WORDS

a	now	said	to
make	pull	the	want(ed)

Houghton Mifflin Harcourt

ending *-ed* /d/

BOOK 81

Tam Yelled

Jen hunted and hunted.
Fox kits rested in a den.
Jen had to be quick! Snap.
Did Jen get a fox picture?
No. The fox kits ran and hid.
Jen went on.

Ducks rested on the sand.
Jen acted fast! Snap.
Did Jen get a duck picture?
No. The ducks swam away.
Jen went on.

A dog and a cat rested on the steps.

Jen acted fast! Snap.

Did Jen get a shot?

Yes! At last Jen has an animal picture.

The hunt is ended!

Jen Hunted

Jen snaps animal pictures.

Will Jen find an animal?

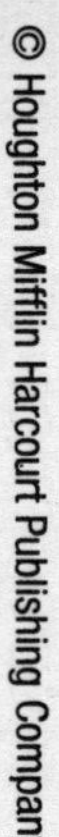

High-Frequency Words Taught to Date

Grade 1

a	cold	friend	her	make	play	take	what
after	come	full	here	many	pull	the	where
all	do	funny	hold	me	put	their	who
and	does	give	how	my	read	they	why
animal	draw	go	I	no	said	to	with
are	eat	good	is	now	see	today	would
away	every	have	like	of	she	too	write
be	far	he	little	one	sing	was	you
blue	find	help	live	our	small	water	
call	for	hear	look	pictures	some	we	

Decoding skills taught to date: consonants *m, s, c, t*; short *a*; consonant *n*; consonant *d*; consonant *p*; consonant *f*; short *i*; consonant *r*; consonant *h*; /z/ spelled *s*; consonant *b*; consonant *g* (hard); short *o*; consonant *l*; consonant *x*; inflection *-s*; short *e*; consonant *y*; consonant *w*; consonant *k*; consonant *v*; consonant *j*; short *u*; /kw/ spelled *qu*; consonant *z*; final consonants *ll*; final consonants *ss*; consonants *ck*; final consonants *ff*; final consonants *zz*; blends with *r*; blends with *l*; blends with *s*; final blend *mp*; final blend *nd*; final blend *nt*; final blend *st*; digraph *th*; ending *-s*; ending *-es*; ending *-ed* /ĕd/

Jen Hunted

DECODABLE WORDS

Target Skill: ending *-ed* /ĕd/

acted	ended	hunted	rested		

Previously Taught Skills

an	did	get	is	quick	steps
and	dog	had	Jen	ran	swam
at	duck	has	kits	run	this
can	ducks	hid	last	sand	went
cat	fast	hunt	not	snap	will
den	fox	in	on	snaps	

SKILLS APPLIED IN WORDS IN STORY: consonants *m, s, c, t*, short *a*; consonant *n*; consonant *d*; consonant *p*; consonant *f*; short *i*; consonant *r*; consonant *h*; /z/ spelled *s*; consonant *g* (hard); short *o*; consonant *l*; consonant *x*; inflection *-s*; short *e*; consonant *w*; consonant *k*; consonant *j*; short *u*; /kw/ spelled *qu*; final consonants *ll*; consonants *ck*; blends with *s*; final blend *st*; final blend *nd*; final blend *nt*; digraph *th*; ending *-s*; ending *-ed* /ĕd/

HIGH-FREQUENCY WORDS

a	find	pictures
animal	no	the
be	picture	to

Houghton Mifflin Harcourt

ending *-ed* /ĕd/

BOOK 80

Jen Hunted

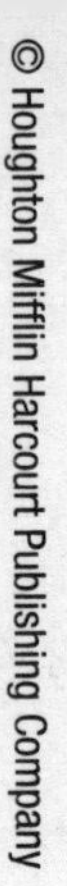

What can foxes eat? Foxes can eat eggs that crack. This fox hunted in grass for eggs.

Bugs can eat plants. Bugs rested on plants and bit, bit, bit them. Rats bit at plants, as well.

What can frogs, foxes, bugs, and rats eat? A lot.

What Can Animals Eat?

What can frogs eat? Frogs can eat bugs. This frog lifted up, up, up and got a bug.

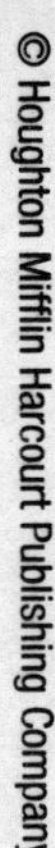

High-Frequency Words Taught to Date

Grade 1

a	cold	friend	her	make	play	take	what
after	come	full	here	many	pull	the	where
all	do	funny	hold	me	put	their	who
and	does	give	how	my	read	they	why
animal	draw	go	I	no	said	to	with
are	eat	good	is	now	see	today	would
away	every	have	like	of	she	too	write
be	far	he	little	one	sing	was	you
blue	find	help	live	our	small	water	
call	for	hear	look	pictures	some	we	

Decoding skills taught to date: consonants *m, s, t,* c; short *a*; consonant *n*; consonant *d*; consonant *p*; consonant *f*; short *i*; consonant *r*; consonant *h*; /z/ spelled *s*; consonant *b*; consonant *g* (hard); short *o*; consonant *l*; consonant *x*, inflection *-s*; short *e*; consonant *y*; consonant *w*; consonant *k*; consonant *v*; consonant *j*; short *u*; /kw/ spelled *qu*; consonant *z*; final consonants *ll*; final consonants *ss*; consonants *ck*; final consonants *ff*; final consonants *zz*; blends with *r*; blends with *l*; blends with *s*; final blend *mp*; final blend *nt*; final blend *nd*; final blend *st*; digraph *th*; ending *-s*; ending *-es*; ending *-ed* /ĕd/

What Can Animals Eat?

DECODABLE WORDS

Target Skill: **ending *-ed* /ĕd/**

hunted	lifted	rested

Previously Taught Skills

and	bugs	frog	lot	that
as	can	frogs	on	them
at	crack	got	plants	this
bit	eggs	grass	rats	up
bug	foxes	in	small	well

SKILLS APPLIED IN WORDS IN STORY: consonants *m, s, c, t*; short *a*; consonant *n*; consonant *d*; consonant *p*; consonant *f*; short *i*; consonant *r*; consonant *h*; /z/ spelled *s*; consonant *b*; consonant *g* (hard); short *o*; consonant *l*; consonant *x*; inflection *-s*; short *e*; consonant *w*; short *u*; final consonants *ll*; final consonants *ss*; final consonant *ck*; blends with *r*; blends with *l*; blends with *s*; final blend *nt*; final blend *nd*; final blend *st*; digraph *th*; ending *-s*; ending *-es*; ending *-ed* /ĕd/

HIGH-FREQUENCY WORDS

a	eat	what
animals	for	

Houghton Mifflin Harcourt.

ending *-ed* /ĕd/

BOOK 79

What Can Animals Eat?

The van is big.
We fill it with boxes.
Then we get kisses and go!
I will miss Dan and Bess.

We stop at last.
Look at the boxes!
This is not fun.
Who can help us now?

Mom! Dad!
Dan and Bess can help!

Pack Up!

My family will pack up today.
Dan and Bess help us fill boxes.
Dad puts in glasses and pans.
Mom packs my trucks and dolls.

High-Frequency Words Taught to Date

Grade 1

a	cold	friend	her	make	play	take	what
after	come	full	here	many	pull	the	where
all	do	funny	hold	me	put	their	who
and	does	give	how	my	read	they	why
animal	draw	go	I	no	said	to	with
are	eat	good	is	now	see	today	would
away	every	have	like	of	she	too	write
be	far	he	little	one	sing	was	you
blue	find	hear	live	our	small	water	
call	for	help	look	pictures	some	we	

Decoding skills taught to date: consonants *m, s, t,* c; short *a*; consonant *n*; consonant *d*; consonant *p*; consonant *f*; short *i*; consonant *r*; consonant *h*; /z/ spelled *s*; consonant *b*; consonant *g* (hard); short *o*; consonant *l*; consonant *x*, inflection *-s*; short *e*; consonant *y*; consonant *w*; consonant *k*; consonant *v*; consonant *j*; short *u*; /kw/ spelled *qu*; consonant *z*; final consonants *ll*; final consonants *ss*; consonants *ck*; final consonants *ff*; final consonants *zz*; blends with *r*; blends with *l*; blends with *s*; final blend *mp*; final blend *nt*; final blend *nd*; final blend *st*; digraph *th*; ending *-s*; ending *-es*

Pack Up!

DECODABLE WORDS

Target Skill: **ending *-es***

boxes	glasses	kisses

Previously Taught Skills

and	Dad	get	miss	pans	up
at	Dan	in	Mom	stop	us
Bess	dolls	is	not	then	van
big	fill	it	pack	this	will
can	fun	last	packs	trucks	with

SKILLS APPLIED IN WORDS IN STORY: consonants *m, s, c, t*; short *a*; consonant *n*; consonant *d*; consonant *p*; consonant *f*; short *i*; consonant *r*; /z/ spelled *s*; consonant *b*; consonant *g* (hard); short *o*; consonant *l*; consonant *x*; inflection -*s*; short *e*; consonant *w*; consonant *k*; consonant *v*; short *u*; final consonants *ll*; final consonants *ss*; consonants *ck*; blends with *r*; blends with *l*; blends with *s*; final blend *st*; digraph *th*; ending -*s*; ending -*es*

HIGH-FREQUENCY WORDS

all	help	my	the	who
family	I	now	today	
go	look	puts	we	

Houghton Mifflin Harcourt

ending *-es*

BOOK 78

Pack Up!

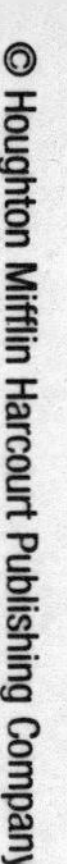

Gram tells the kids not to look in the boxes yet.
Then Gram kisses Glen and Beth.
Glen and Beth like kisses from Gram.

Mom spots Glen and Beth with the boxes.
Glen asks, "Can we look in them?"
Mom nods yes.

Glen and Beth got glass animals!
"Gram got us foxes," Glen tells Mom.
"Gram put foxes in the boxes!"

Gram Gives Us Boxes

Gram has boxes for the kids.
She hands a box to Glen and a box to Beth.
"What is this?" they ask.

High-Frequency Words Taught to Date

Grade 1

a	cold	friend	her	make	play	take	what
after	come	full	here	many	pull	the	where
all	do	funny	hold	me	put	their	who
and	does	give	how	my	read	they	why
animal	draw	go	I	no	said	to	with
are	eat	good	is	now	see	today	would
away	every	have	like	of	she	too	write
be	far	he	little	one	sing	was	you
blue	find	hear	live	our	small	water	
call	for	help	look	pictures	some	we	

Decoding skills taught to date: consonants *m, s, t, c*; short *a*; consonant *n*; consonant *d*; consonant *p*; consonant *f*; short *i*; consonant *r*; consonant *h*; /z/ spelled *s*; consonant *b*; consonant *g* (hard); short *o*; consonant *l*; consonant *x*, inflection *-s*; short *e*; consonant *y*; consonant *w*; consonant *k*; consonant *v*; consonant *j*; short *u*; /kw/ spelled *qu*; consonant *z*; final consonants *ll*; final consonants *ss*; consonants *ck*; final consonants *ff*; final consonants *zz*; blends with *r*; blends with *l*; blends with *s*; final blend *mp*; final blend *nt*; final blend *nd*; final blend *st*; digraph *th*; ending *-s*; ending *-es*

Gram Gives Us Boxes

DECODABLE WORDS

Target Skill: **ending *-es***

boxes	foxes	kisses

Previously Taught Skills

and	can	Gram	kids	tells	with
ask	from	hands	Mom	them	yes
asks	glass	has	nods	then	yet
Beth	Glen	in	not	this	
box	got	is	spots	us	

SKILLS APPLIED IN WORDS IN STORY: consonants *m, s, c, t,* short *a*; consonant *n*; consonant *d*; consonant *p*; consonant *f*; short *i*; consonant *r*; consonant *h*; /z/ spelled *s*; consonant *b*; consonant *g* (hard); short *o*; consonant *x*; inflection *-s*; short *e*; consonant *y*; consonant *w*; consonant *k*; short *u*; final consonants *ll*; final consonants *ss*; blends with *r*; blends with *l*; blends with *s*; final blend *nd*; digraph *th*; ending *-s*; ending *-es*

HIGH-FREQUENCY WORDS

a	gives	put	they	what
animals	like	she	to	
for	look	the	we	

Houghton Mifflin Harcourt.

ending *-es*

BOOK 77

Gram Gives Us Boxes

"Jon is back at last," Kim tells his pals.
The pals can see his trip in pictures!
They see big, big rocks and lots of sand.
But they do not spot Jon.

"Jon, we can spot hills, rocks, and sand.
But are **you** in the pictures?" asks Kim.

"Here I am," Jon tells his pals.
At last his pals spot him!
Jon is in the water!

Jon on a Trip

Jon will go on a trip.
Jon gets on his bus.
"Have fun, Jon!" calls Kim.

High-Frequency Words Taught to Date

Grade 1

a	cold	friend	her	make	play	take	what
after	come	full	here	many	pull	the	where
all	do	funny	hold	me	put	their	who
and	does	give	how	my	read	they	why
animal	draw	go	I	no	said	to	with
are	eat	good	is	now	see	today	would
away	every	have	like	of	she	too	write
be	far	he	little	one	sing	was	you
blue	find	help	live	our	small	water	
call	for	hear	look	pictures	some	we	

Decoding skills taught to date: consonants *m, s, t,* c; short *a*; consonant *n*; consonant *d*; consonant *p*; consonant *f*; short *i*; consonant *r*; consonant *h*; /z/ spelled *s*; consonant *b*; consonant *g* (hard); short *o*; consonant *l*; consonant *x*, inflection *-s*; short *e*; consonant *y*; consonant *w*; consonant *k*; consonant *v*; consonant *j*; short *u*; /kw/ spelled *qu*; consonant *z*; final consonants *ll*; final consonants *ss*; consonants *ck*; final consonants *ff*; final consonants *zz*; blends with *r*; blends with *l*; blends with *s*; final blend *mp*; final blend *nt*; final blend *nd*; final blend *st*; digraph *th*; ending *-s*

Jon on a Trip

DECODABLE WORDS

Target Skill: **ending *-s***

hills	pals	rocks

Previously Taught Skills

am	big	gets	Jon	on	trip
and	bus	him	Kim	pals	will
asks	but	his	last	sand	
at	can	in	lots	spot	
back	fun	is	not	tells	

SKILLS APPLIED IN WORDS IN STORY: consonants *m, s, t*; short *a*; consonant *n*; consonant *p*; consonant *f*; short *i*; consonant *r*; consonant *h*; /z/ spelled *s*; consonant *b*; consonant *g* (hard); short *o*; consonant *l*; inflection *-s*; short *e*; consonant *w*; consonant *k*; consonant *j*; short *u*; final consonants *ll*; consonants *ck*; blends with *r*; blends with *s*; final blend *nd*; final blend *st*; ending *-s*

HIGH-FREQUENCY WORDS

a	go	of	they
are	have	pictures	water
calls	here	see	we
do	I	the	you

Houghton Mifflin Harcourt

ending *-s*

BOOK 76

Jon on a Trip

Ted helps ducks, too.
He will help the ducks swim.

Meg is a vet.
Meg helps big animals.
She will help a black
ram jump.

Mack sits still.
Meg pulls on quills.
Mack is glad Meg helps him.

Vets Help Animals

Ted is a vet.
Ted helps little animals.
He helps cats and pups.

High-Frequency Words Taught to Date

Grade 1

a	cold	friend	her	make	play	take	what
after	come	full	here	many	pull	the	where
all	do	funny	hold	me	put	their	who
and	does	give	how	my	read	they	why
animal	draw	go	I	no	said	to	with
are	eat	good	is	now	see	today	would
away	every	have	like	of	she	too	write
be	far	he	little	one	sing	was	you
blue	find	hear	live	our	small	water	
call	for	help	look	pictures	some	we	

Decoding skills taught to date: consonants *m, s, t;* c, short *a*; consonant *n;* consonant *d*; consonant *p*; consonant *f*; short *i*; consonant *r*; consonant *h;* /z/ spelled *s*; consonant *b;* consonant *g* (hard); short *o*; consonant *l;* consonant *x*; inflection *-s*; short *e*; consonant *y;* consonant *w;* consonant *k;* consonant *v;* consonant *j*; short *u*; /kw/ spelled *qu*; consonant *z*; final consonants *ll;* final consonants *ss;* consonants *ck*; final consonants *ff;* final consonants *zz*; blends with *r;* blends with *l;* blends with *s*; final blend *mp;* final blend *nt;* final blend *nd;* final blend *st*; digraph *th*; ending *-s*

Vets Help Animals

DECODABLE WORDS

Target Skill: **ending *-s***

cats	pups	vets
ducks	quills	

Previously Taught Skills

big	him	Meg	swim
black	is	on	Ted
glad	jump	ram	vet
help	Mack	still	will

SKILLS APPLIED IN WORDS IN STORY: consonants *m, s, c, t*; short *a*; consonant *n*; consonant *d*; consonant *p*; short *i*; consonant *r*; consonant *h*; /z/ spelled *s*; consonant *b*; consonant *g* (hard); short *o*; consonant *l*; inflection *-s*; short *e*; consonant *w*; consonant *v*; consonant *j*; short *u*; /kw/ spelled *qu*; final consonants *ll*; consonants *ck*; blends with *l*; blends with *s*; final blend *mp*; ending *-s*

HIGH-FREQUENCY WORDS

a	animal(s)	help	pulls	the
and	he	little	she	too

Houghton Mifflin Harcourt

ending *-s*

BOOK 75

Vets Help Animals

The cloth cat slips.
It is not in his hands.
It drops far.

Thud! The cloth cat fell
on the path.
Will Thad pick up
his friend?

Thad is not fast.
But he gets his cloth cat
off the path.
Now the cloth cat must
have a bath!

Thad and His Cloth Cat

Thad is a sloth.
He naps with his little
cloth cat.

High-Frequency Words Taught to Date

Grade 1

a	cold	friend	her	make	play	take	what
after	come	full	here	many	pull	the	where
all	do	funny	hold	me	put	their	who
and	does	give	how	my	read	they	why
animal	draw	go	I	no	said	to	with
are	eat	good	is	now	see	today	would
away	every	have	like	of	she	too	write
be	far	he	little	one	sing	was	you
blue	find	hear	live	our	small	water	
call	for	help	look	pictures	some	we	

Decoding skills taught to date: consonants *m, s, c, t*; short *a*; consonant *n*; consonant *d*; consonant *p*; consonant *f*; short *i*; consonant *r*; consonant *h*; /z/ spelled *s*; consonant *b*; consonant *g* (hard); short *o*; consonant *l*; consonant *x*; inflection *-s*; short *e*; consonant *y*; consonant *w*; consonant *k*; consonant *v*; consonant *j*; short *u*; /kw/ spelled *qu*; consonant *z*; final consonants *ll*; final consonants *ss*; consonants *ck*; final consonants *ff*; final consonants *zz*; blends with *r*; blends with *l*; blends with *s*; final blend *mp*; final blend *nt*; final blend *nd*; final blend *st*; digraph *th*

Thad and His Cloth Cat

DECODABLE WORDS

Target Skill: **digraph *th***

bath	path	Thad	with
cloth	sloth	thud	

Previously Taught Skills

and	fell	in	naps	pick
cat	gets	is	not	slips
drops	hands	it	off	up
fast	his	must	on	will

SKILLS APPLIED IN WORDS IN STORY: consonants *m, s, c, t*; short *a*; consonant *n*; consonant *d*; consonant *p*; consonant *f*; short *i*; consonant *r*; consonant *h*; /z/ spelled *s*; consonant *b*; consonant *g* (hard); short *o*; consonant *l*; inflection *-s*; short *e*; consonant *w*; short *u*; final consonants *ll*; consonants *ck*; final consonants *ff*; blends with *r*; blends with *l*; final blend *nd*; final blend *st*

HIGH-FREQUENCY WORDS

a	friend	he	now
far	have	little	the

Houghton Mifflin Harcourt

digraph *th*

BOOK 74

Thad and His Cloth Cat

"The cloth rips," said Bob.
"It is a bit thin, thin, thin."

Liz has the best top.
It is not thick. It is not thin.
It is for Bob.

"A moth is on the cloth!" said Bob.
"Yum, yum, yum," said the moth.

Moth on the Cloth

"The top is hot," said Bob.
"The cloth is thick, thick, thick."

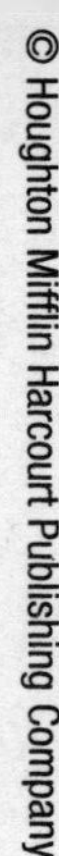

High-Frequency Words Taught to Date

Grade 1

a	cold	friend	her	make	play	take	what
after	come	full	here	many	pull	the	where
all	do	funny	hold	me	put	their	who
and	does	give	how	my	read	they	why
animal	draw	go	I	no	said	to	with
are	eat	good	is	now	see	today	would
away	every	have	like	of	she	too	write
be	far	he	little	one	sing	was	you
blue	find	hear	live	our	small	water	
call	for	help	look	pictures	some	we	

Decoding skills taught to date: consonants *m, s, t, c,* short *a*; consonant *n*; consonant *d*; consonant *p*; consonant *f*; short *i*; consonant *r*; consonant *h*; /z/ spelled *s*; consonant *b*; consonant *g* (hard); *short o*; consonant *l*; consonant *x*; inflection *-s*; short *e*; consonant *y*; consonant *w*; consonant *k*; consonant *v*; consonant *j*; short *u*; /kw/ spelled *qu*; consonant *z*; final consonants *ll*; final consonants *ss*; consonants *ck*; final consonants *ff*; final consonants *zz*; blends with *r*; blend with *l*; blends with *s*; final blend *mp*; final blend *nt*; final blend *nd*; final blend *st*; digraph *th*

Moth on the Cloth

DECODABLE WORDS

Target Skill: **digraph *th***

cloth	moth	thick	thin	

Previously Taught Skills

bit	has	it	on	yum
best	hot	Liz	rips	
Bob	is	not	top	

SKILLS APPLIED IN WORDS IN STORY: consonants *m, s, t, c,* short *a;* consonant *n*; consonant *p*; short *i*; consonant *r*; consonant *h*; /z/ spelled *s*; consonant *b*; short *o*; consonant *l*; inflection -*s*; short *e*; consonant *y*; short *u*; consonants *ck*; blends with *l*; final blend *st*

HIGH-FREQUENCY WORDS

a	for	said	the

Houghton Mifflin Harcourt

digraph *th*

BOOK 73

Moth on the Cloth

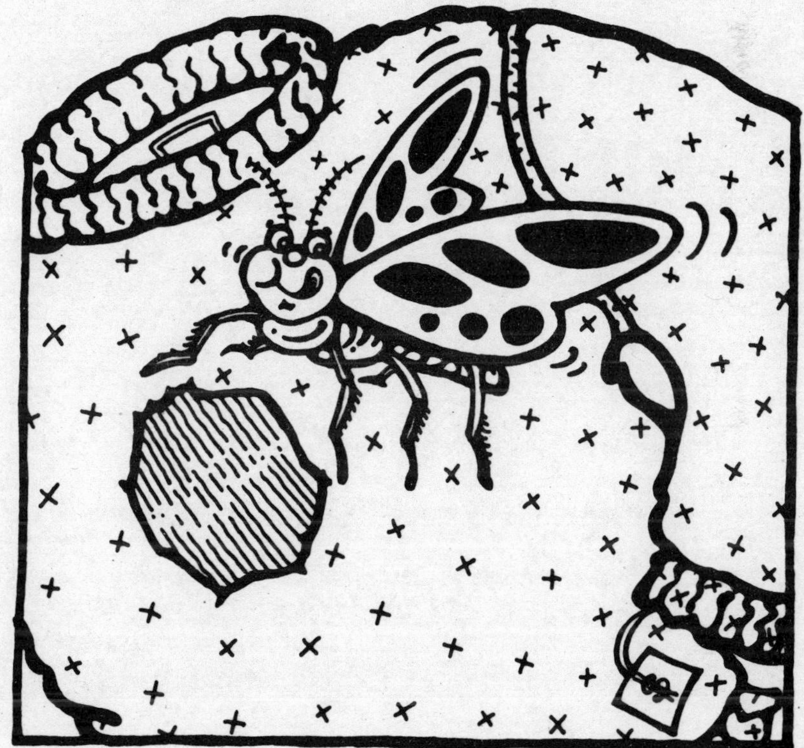

Jill has fun at camp.
She runs up the ramp.

Jill runs as fast as she can.
She runs past Bess.
Will Jill run past Ben?

Jill did not get past Ben.
Jill tells Ben, "I did my best,
but you just run too fast!
Now we can rest!"

Jill at Camp

Jill is glad to go to camp.
She will get on a bus.
Jill gives Dad a big hug.

High-Frequency Words Taught to Date

Grade 1

a	do	give	how	now	see	too
after	does	go	I	of	she	was
all	draw	good	is	one	sing	we
and	eat	have	like	our	small	what
animal	every	he	look	pictures	some	who
are	find	hear	make	play	take	why
away	for	help	many	pull	the	with
be	friend	her	me	put	they	would
call	full	here	my	read	to	write
come	funny	hold	no	said	today	you

Decoding skills taught to date: consonants *m, s, t,* c; short *a*; consonant *n*; consonant *d*; consonant *p*; consonant *f*; short *i*; consonant *r*; consonant *h*; /z/ spelled *s*; consonant *b*; consonant *g* (hard); short *o*; consonant *l*; consonant *x*, inflection *-s*; short *e*; consonant *y*; consonant *w*; consonant *k*; consonant *v*; consonant *j*; short *u*; /kw/ spelled *qu*; consonant *z*; final consonants *ll*; final consonants *ss*; consonants *ck;* final consonants *ff*; final consonants *zz*; blends with *r*; blends with *l*; blends with *s*; final blend *mp*; final blend *nt*; final blend *nd*; final blend *st*

Jill at Camp

DECODABLE WORDS

Target Skill: **final blend *st***

best	fast	just	past	rest	

Previously Taught Skills

as	bus	did	hug	ramp	will
at	but	fun	is	run	
Ben	camp	get	Jill	runs	
Bess	can	glad	not	tells	
big	Dad	has	on	up	

SKILLS APPLIED IN WORDS IN STORY: consonants *s, t, c*; short *a*; consonant *n*; consonant *d*; consonant *p*; consonant *f*; short *i*; consonant *r*; consonant *h*; /z/ spelled *s*; consonant *b*; consonant *g* (hard); short *o*; inflection *-s*; short *e*; consonant *w*; consonant *j*; short *u*; final consonants *ll*; final consonants *ss*; blends with *l*; final blend *mp*

HIGH-FREQUENCY WORDS

a	I	she	too
gives	my	the	we
go	now	to	you

Houghton Mifflin Harcourt

final blend *st*

BOOK 72

Jill at Camp

Jeff spots the vest on the rack.
Can Jeff jump up and get it?
Jump up, Jeff! Jump up!

Yes! Jeff grabs it.
"It was just up here on a peg,"
said Jeff.

Lin has her best vest back.
Jeff did it!
Lin is glad at last.

Jeff Spots It

"My vest is not in here!" said Lin.
"My best vest is not in here!"
Can you spot her vest?

High-Frequency Words Taught to Date

Grade 1

a	come	full	her	many	play	some	what
after	do	funny	here	me	pull	take	who
all	does	give	hold	my	put	the	why
and	draw	go	how	no	read	they	with
animal	eat	good	I	now	said	to	would
are	every	have	is	of	see	today	write
away	find	he	like	one	she	too	you
be	for	hear	look	our	sing	was	
call	friend	help	make	pictures	small	we	

Decoding skills taught to date: consonants *m, s, t, c*; short *a*; consonant *n*; consonant *d*; consonant *p*; consonant *f*; short *i*; consonant *r*; consonant *h*; /z/ spelled *s*; consonant *b*; consonant *g* (hard); short *o*; consonant *l*; consonant *x*, inflection *-s*; short *e*; consonant *y*; consonant *w*; consonant *k*; consonant *v*; consonant *j*; short *u*; /kw/ spelled *qu*; consonant *z*; final consonants *ll*; final consonants *ss*; consonants *ck*; final consonants *ff*; final consonants *zz*; blends with *r*; blends with *l*; blends with *s*; final blend *mp*; final blend *nt*; final blend *nd*; final blend *st*

Jeff Spots It

DECODABLE WORDS

Target Skill: **final blend *st***

best last
just vest

Previously Taught Skills

at	glad	it	on	up
back	grabs	Jeff	peg	yes
can	has	jump	rack	
did	in	Lin	spot	
get	is	not	spots	

SKILLS APPLIED IN WORDS IN STORY: consonants *s, c, t,* short *a;* consonant *n;* consonant *d;* consonant *p;* short *i;* consonant *h;* /z/ spelled *s;* consonant *b;* consonant *g* (hard); short *o;* consonant *l;* inflection *-s;* short *e;* consonant *y;* consonant *v;* consonant *j;* short *u;* consonants *ck;* final consonants *ff;* blends with *r;* blends with *l;* blends with *s;* final blend *mp*

HIGH-FREQUENCY WORDS

a	her	my	the	you
and	here	said	was	

Houghton Mifflin Harcourt.

final blend *st*

BOOK 71

Jeff Spots It

Lin can make a hand print
in the sand.

Lin finds a big ant.
It is in the sand, too.

Lin sees Rand at the pond!
Lin and Rand can run and
have fun in the sand.
Sand is fun!

Sand, Sand, Sand

Lin is at the pond.
Mom and Dad set up camp.
Lin sits in the sand.

High-Frequency Words Taught to Date

Grade 1

a	come	full	her	many	play	some	what
after	do	funny	here	me	pull	take	who
all	does	give	hold	my	put	the	why
and	draw	go	how	no	read	they	with
animal	eat	good	I	now	said	to	would
are	every	have	is	of	see	today	write
away	find	he	like	one	she	too	you
be	for	hear	look	our	sing	was	
call	friend	help	make	pictures	small	we	

Decoding skills taught to date: consonants *m, s, c, t*; short *a*; consonant *n*; consonant *d*; consonant *p*; consonant *f*; short *i*; consonant *r*; consonant *h*; /z/ spelled *s*; consonant *b*; consonant *g* (hard); short *o*; consonant *l*; consonant *x*; inflection *-s*; short *e*; consonant *y*; consonant *w*; consonant *k*; consonant *v*; consonant *j*; short *u*; /kw/ spelled *qu*; consonant *z*; final consonants *ll*; final consonants *ss*; consonants *-ck*; final consonants *ff*; final consonants *zz*; blends with *r*; blends with *l*; blends with *s*; final blend *mp*; final blend *nt*; final blend *nd*

Sand, Sand, Sand

DECODABLE WORDS

Target Skill: **final blend *nd***

and	pond	sand
hand	Rand	

Previously Taught Skills

ant	can	is	print	up
at	Dad	it	run	
big	fun	Lin	set	
camp	in	Mom	sits	

SKILLS APPLIED IN WORDS IN STORY: consonants *m, s, c, t*; short *a*; consonant *n*; consonant *d*; consonant *p*; consonant *f*; short *i*; consonant *r*; consonant *h*; /z/ spelled *s*; consonant *b*; consonant *g* (hard); short *o*; consonant *l*; inflection *-s*; short *e*; short *u*; blends with *r*; final blend *mp*; final blend *nt*; final blend *nd*

HIGH-FREQUENCY WORDS

a	have	sees	too
finds	make	the	

Houghton Mifflin Harcourt

final blend *nd*

BOOK 70

Sand, Sand, Sand

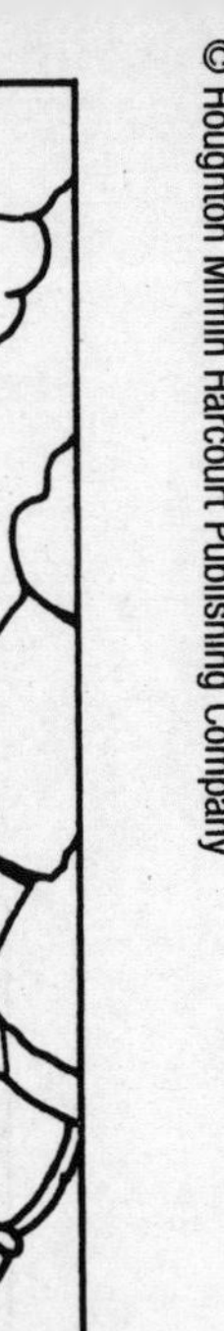

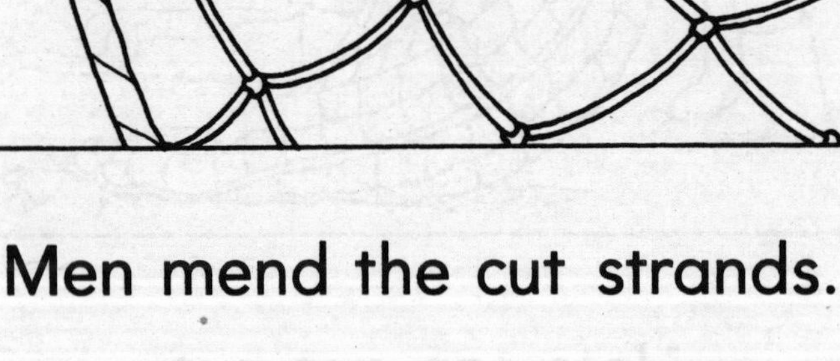

Men mend the cut strands.

Wind sends the damp net up. "Quick, lend a hand!" yells the blond man.

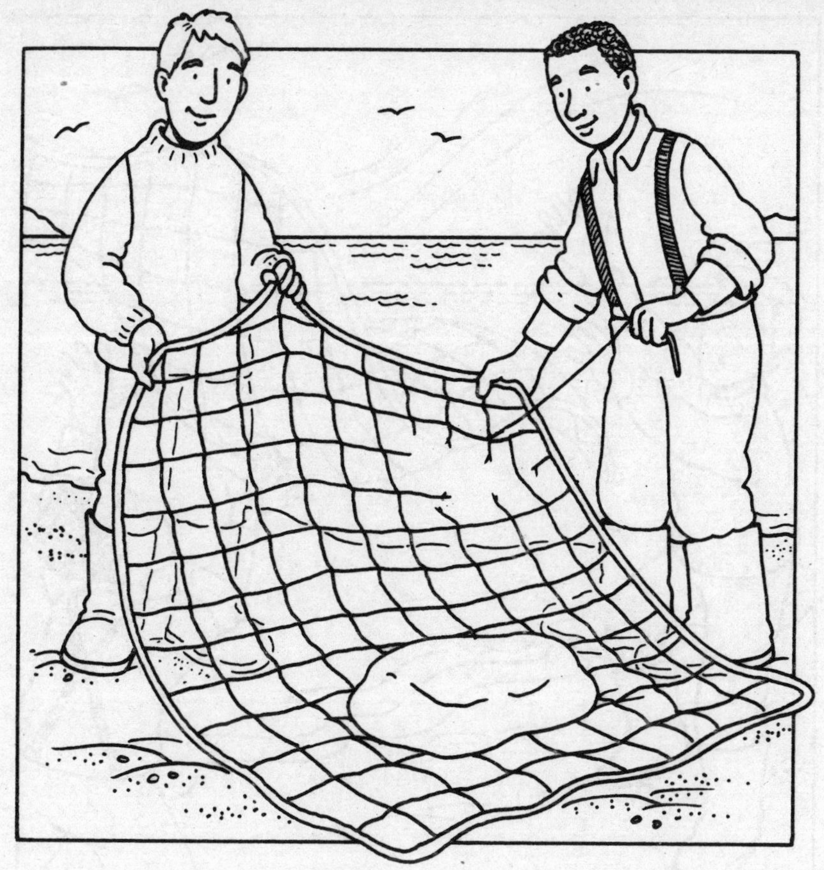

A rock gets the net flat.
Men stand on land and
mend, mend, mend.

Mend, Mend, Mend

Nets can get cut.

High-Frequency Words Taught to Date

Grade 1

a	come	full	her	many	play	some	what
after	do	funny	here	me	pull	take	who
all	does	give	hold	my	put	the	why
and	draw	go	how	no	read	they	with
animal	eat	good	I	now	said	to	would
are	every	have	is	of	see	today	write
away	find	he	like	one	she	too	you
be	for	hear	look	our	sing	was	
call	friend	help	make	pictures	small	we	

Decoding skills taught to date: consonants *m, s, c, t*; short *a*; consonant *n*; consonant *d*; consonant *p*; consonant *f*; short *i*; consonant *r*; consonant *h*; final /z/ spelled *s*; consonant *b*; consonant *g* (hard); short *o*; consonant *l*; consonant *x*; inflection *-s*; short *e*; consonant *y*; consonant *w*; consonant *k*; consonant *v*; consonant *j*; short *u*; /kw/ spelled *qu*; consonant *z*; double final consonants *ll*; double final consonants *ss*; consonants *-ck*; double final consonants *ff*; double final consonants *zz*; blends with *r*; blends with *l*; blends with *s*; final blend *mp*; final blend *nt*; final blend *nd*

Mend, Mend, Mend

DECODABLE WORDS

Target Skill: **final blend *nd***

and	hand	lend	sends	strands
blond	land	mend	stand	wind

Previously Taught Skills

can	flat	man	nets	rock
cut	get	men	on	up
damp	gets	net	quick	yells

SKILLS APPLIED IN WORDS IN STORY: consonants *m, s, c, t*; short *a*; consonant *n*; consonant *d*; consonant *f*; short *i*; consonant *r*; consonant *h*; consonant *b*; consonant *g* (hard); short *o*; consonant *l*; inflection *-s*; short *e*; consonant *y*; consonant *w*; consonant *k*; short *u*; /kw/ spelled *qu*; final consonants *ll*; consonants *-ck*; blends with *r*; blends with *l*; blends with *s*; final blend *mp*; final blend *nd*

HIGH-FREQUENCY WORDS

a	the

Houghton Mifflin Harcourt

final blend *nd*

BOOK 69

Mend, Mend, Mend

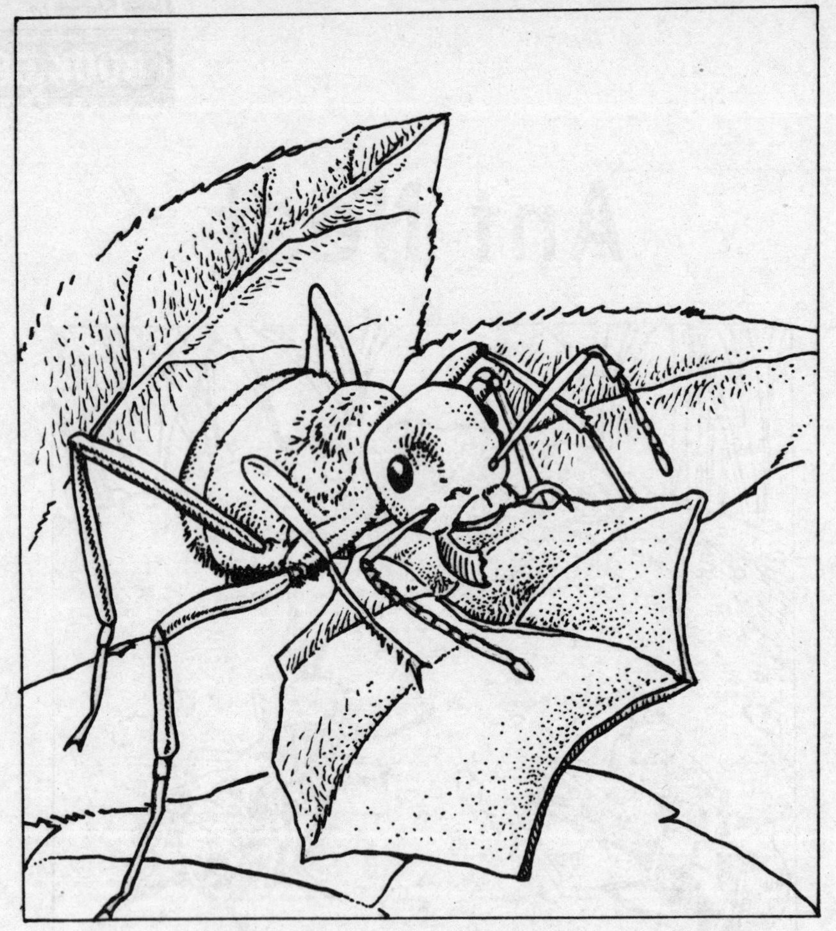

Ants hunt for plants.
Ants take bits back
to ants in the nest.
Hunt, ant, hunt!

If a nest has a dent,
ants fix it up.

One ant is the mom.
Mom is big.
Small ants help Mom.

Ants do lots and lots!

final blend *nt*

BOOK 68

Ant Nest

Ants can do a lot!
An ant nest has a vent.
Ants go in it.

High-Frequency Words Taught to Date

Grade 1

a	come	full	her	many	play	some	what
after	do	funny	here	me	pull	take	who
all	does	give	hold	my	put	the	why
and	draw	go	how	no	read	they	with
animal	eat	good	I	now	said	to	would
are	every	have	is	of	see	today	write
away	find	he	like	one	she	too	you
be	for	hear	look	our	sing	was	
call	friend	help	make	pictures	small	we	

Decoding skills taught to date: consonants *m, s, c, t*; short *a*; consonant *n*; consonant *d*; consonant *p*; consonant *f*; short *i*; consonant *r*; consonant *h*; final /z/ spelled *s*; consonant *b*; consonant *g* (hard); short *o*; consonant *l*; consonant *x*; inflection *-s*; short *e*; consonant *y*; consonant *w*; consonant *k*; consonant *v*; consonant *j*; short *u*; /kw/ spelled *qu*; consonant *z*; double final consonants *ll*; double final consonants *ss*; consonants *-ck*; double final consonants *ff*; double final consonants *zz*; blends with *r*; blends with *l*; blends with *s*; final blend *mp*; final blend *nt*

Ant Nest

DECODABLE WORDS

Target Skill: **final blend *nt***

ant	dent	plants
ants	hunt	vent

Previously Taught Skills

an	can	if	lot
back	fix	in	mom
big	has	is	nest
bits	help	it	up

SKILLS APPLIED IN WORDS IN STORY: consonants *m, s, c, t*; short *a*; consonant *n*; consonant *d*; consonant *p*; consonant *f*; short *i*; consonant *h*; final /z/ spelled *s*; consonant *b*; consonant *g* (hard); short *o*; consonant *l*; consonant *x*; inflection *-s*; short *e*; consonant *w*; consonant *k*; consonant *v*; short *u*; consonants *-ck*; blends with *l*; blends with *s*; final blend *nt*

HIGH-FREQUENCY WORDS

a	do	go	small	the
and	for	one	take	to

Houghton Mifflin Harcourt.

final blend *nt*

BOOK 68

Ant Nest

Kent set up his tent.
A tent stick was bent.
It had a bad dent.

Kent went back to Rent a Tent.
"The tent stick is bent. It has
a bad dent," said Kent.
Kent got a good tent stick.

Kent went back with his good tent stick.
He set up his tent and went in!
Kent had fun!

final blend *nt*

BOOK 67

Rent a Tent, Kent

Kent went to rent a tent at Rent a Tent.

High-Frequency Words Taught to Date

Grade 1

a	come	full	her	many	play	some	what
after	do	funny	here	me	pull	take	who
all	does	give	hold	my	put	the	why
and	draw	go	how	no	read	they	with
animal	eat	good	I	now	said	to	would
are	every	have	is	of	see	today	write
away	find	he	like	one	she	too	you
be	for	hear	look	our	sing	was	
call	friend	help	make	pictures	small	we	

Decoding skills taught to date: consonants *m, s, c, t*; short *a*; consonant *n*; consonant *d*; consonant *p*; consonant *f*; short *i*; consonant *r*; consonant *h*; /z/ spelled *s*; consonant *b*; consonant *g* (hard); short *o*; consonant *l*; consonant *x*; inflection *-s*; short *e*; consonant *y*; consonant *w*; consonant *k*; consonant *v*; consonant *j*; short *u*; /kw/ spelled *qu*; consonant *z*; final consonants *ll*; final consonants *ss*; consonants *-ck*; final consonants *ff*; final consonants *zz*; blends with *r*; blends with *l*; blends with *s*; final blend *mp*; final blend *nt*

Rent a Tent, Kent

DECODABLE WORDS

Target Skill: **final blend *nt***

bent	Kent	tent
dent	rent	went

Previously Taught Skills

at	fun	has	is	stick
back	got	his	it	up
bad	had	in	set	

SKILLS APPLIED IN WORDS IN STORY: consonants *s, c, t*; short *a*; consonant *n*; consonant *d*; consonant *p*; consonant *f*; short *i*; consonant *r*; consonant *h*; /z/ spelled *s*; consonant *b*; consonant *g* (hard); short *o*; consonant *w*; short *e*; consonant *k*; short *u*; consonants *-ck*; blends with *s*; final blend *nt*

HIGH-FREQUENCY WORDS

a	good	said	to	with
and	he	the	was	

Houghton Mifflin Harcourt.

final blend *nt*

BOOK 67

Rent a Tent, Kent

The pig is in a pen.
The pen has damp mud in it.
Pigs can dig in damp mud.
What can pigs find in mud?

Pigs can play.
Pigs can romp and stomp in damp mud.

If a pig is hot, it sits in mud.
The pen is a good spot for pigs.

Pigs

The pig is a big, plump animal.

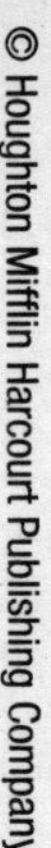

High-Frequency Words Taught to Date

Grade 1

a
after
all
and
animal
are
away
be
call
come
do
does
draw
eat
every
find
for
friend
full
funny
give
go
good
have
he
hear
help
her
here
hold
how
I
is
like
look
make
many
me
my
no
now
of
one
our
pictures
play
pull
put
read
said
see
she
sing
small
some
take
the
they
to
today
too
was
we
what
who
why
with
would
write
you

Decoding skills taught to date: consonants *m, s, t, c*; short *a*; consonant *n*; consonant *d*; consonant *p*; consonant *f*; short *i*; consonant *r*; consonant *h*; consonant *s* /z/; consonant *b*; consonant *g* (hard); short *o*; consonant *l*; consonant *x*, inflection *-s*; short *e*; consonant *y*; consonant *w*; consonant *k*; consonant *v*; consonant *j*; short *u*; /kw/ spelled *qu*; consonant *z*; double final consonants *ll*; double final consonants *ss*; consonants *ck*; double final consonants *ff*; double final consonants *zz*; blends with *r*; blends with *l*; blends with *s*; final blend *mp*

Pigs

DECODABLE WORDS

Target Skill: **final blend *mp***

damp	romp
plump	stomp

Previously Taught Skills

big	has	in	mud	pigs
can	hot	is	pen	sits
dig	if	it	pig	spot

SKILLS APPLIED IN WORDS IN STORY: consonants *m, s, c, t,* short *a;* consonant *n;* consonant *d;* consonant *p;* consonant *f;* short *i;* consonant *r;* consonant *h;* consonant *s /z/;* consonant *b;* consonant *g* (hard)*;* short *o;* consonant *l;* inflection *-s;* short *e;* short *u;* blends with *s;* blends with *l;* final blend *mp*

HIGH-FREQUENCY WORDS

a	animal	for	play	what
and	find	good	the	

Houghton Mifflin Harcourt

final blend *mp*

BOOK 66

Pigs

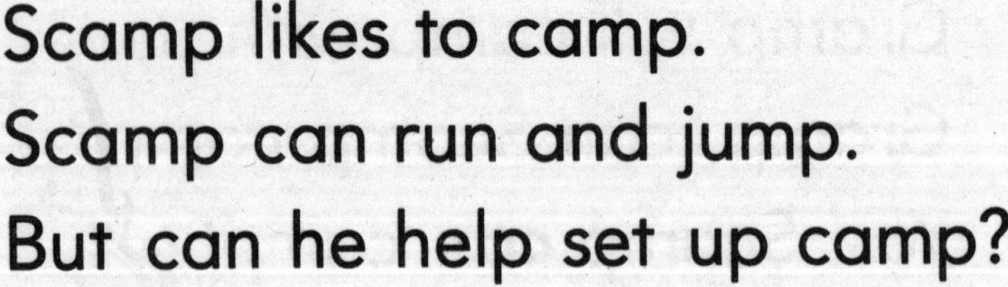

Scamp likes to camp.
Scamp can run and jump.
But can he help set up camp?

Scamp can jump up on a stump.
But will he help set up camp?

Scamp can run and jump.
But Scamp can set up camp, too!
Scamp **likes** to camp.

final blend *mp*

BOOK 65

Scamp at Camp

We like to camp.
Gramp will camp with us.
Gramp, can Scamp camp?
Yes, Scamp **can** camp!
Get in, Scamp!

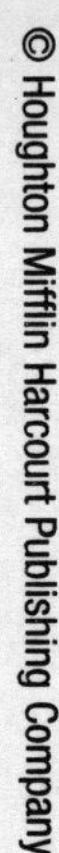

High-Frequency Words Taught to Date

Grade 1

a	come	full	her	many	play	some	what
after	do	funny	here	me	pull	take	who
all	does	give	hold	my	put	the	why
and	draw	go	how	no	read	they	with
animal	eat	good	I	now	said	to	would
are	every	have	is	of	see	today	write
away	find	he	like	one	she	too	you
be	for	hear	look	our	sing	was	
call	friend	help	make	pictures	small	we	

Decoding skills taught to date: consonants *m, s, t, c*; short *a*; consonant *n*; consonant *d*; consonant *p*; consonant *f*; short *i*; consonant *r*; consonant *h*; consonant *s* /z/; consonant *b*; consonant *g* (hard); short *o*; consonant *l*; consonant *x*, inflection *-s*; short *e*; consonant *y*; consonant *w*; consonant *k*; consonant *v*; consonant *j*; short *u*; /kw/ spelled *qu*; consonant *z*; double final consonants *ll*; double final consonants *ss*; consonants *ck*; double final consonants *ff*; double final consonants *zz*; blends with *r*; blends with *l*; blends with *s*; final blend *mp*

Scamp at Camp

DECODABLE WORDS

Target Skill: **final blend *mp***

camp	jump	stump
Gramp	Scamp	

Previously Taught Skills

at	get	run	us
but	in	set	will
can	on	up	yes

SKILLS APPLIED IN WORDS IN STORY: consonants *m, s, c, t,* short *a*; consonant *n*; consonant *p*; short *i*; consonant *r*; consonant *b*; consonant *g* (hard); short *o*; short *e*; consonant *y*; consonant *w*; consonant *j*; short *u*; double final consonants *ll*; blends with *s*; final blend *mp*

HIGH-FREQUENCY WORDS

a	he	like	to	we
and	help	likes	too	with

Houghton Mifflin Harcourt.

final blend *mp*

BOOK 65

Scamp at Camp

Will Spot snag the snack?

Stop, Spot! Stop, stop, stop!

Do not be sad, Spot.
Have a dog snack!

Spot Smells a Snack

Spot can smell a snack.
Sniff, sniff, sniff.

High-Frequency Words Taught to Date

Grade 1

a	call	friend	help	look	our	sing	we
after	come	full	her	make	pictures	some	what
all	do	funny	here	many	play	the	who
and	does	go	hold	me	pull	they	why
animal	draw	good	how	my	read	to	with
are	every	have	I	no	said	today	would
away	find	he	is	now	see	too	write
be	for	hear	like	of	she	was	you

Decoding skills taught to date: consonants *m, s, c, t*; short *a*; consonant *n*; consonant *d*; consonant *p*; consonant *f*; short *i*; consonant *r*; consonant *h*; /z/ spelled *s*; consonant *b*; consonant *g* (hard); short *o*; consonant *l*; consonant *x*; inflection *-s*; short *e*; consonant *y*; consonant *w*; consonant *k*; consonant *v*; consonant *j*; short *u*; /kw/ spelled *qu*; consonant *z*; final consonants *ll*; final consonants *ss*; consonants *-ck*; final consonants *ff*; final consonants *zz*; blends with *r*; blends with *l*; blends with *s*

Spot Smells a Snack

DECODABLE WORDS

Target Skill: **blends with *s***

smell	snack	sniff	stop
smells	snag	Spot	

Previously Taught Skills

can	not	will
dog	sad	

SKILLS APPLIED IN WORDS IN STORY: consonants *m, s, c, t*; short *a*; consonant *n*; consonant *d*; consonant *p*; consonant *f*; short *i*; consonant *h*; /z/ spelled *s*; consonant *b*; consonant *g*; short *o*; consonant *l*; inflection *-s*; short *e*; consonant *w*; consonant *k*; final consonants *ll*; consonants *-ck*; final consonants *ff*; blends with *s*

HIGH-FREQUENCY WORDS

a	do	the
be	have	

Houghton Mifflin Harcourt.

blends with *s*

BOOK 64

Spot Smells a Snack

The spot is flat.
The sled is still stuck.

The hill is slick.
Now Stan can sled.

Stan slid and sped on his sled.

Stan Sleds

Stan has a sled.
It does not slip.

High-Frequency Words Taught to Date

Grade 1

a	call	friend	help	look	our	sing	we
after	come	full	her	make	pictures	some	what
all	do	funny	here	many	play	the	who
and	does	go	hold	me	pull	they	why
animal	draw	good	how	my	read	to	with
are	every	have	I	no	said	today	would
away	find	he	is	now	see	too	write
be	for	hear	like	of	she	was	you

Decoding skills taught to date: consonants *m, s, c, t*; short *a*; consonant *n*; consonant *d*; consonant *p*; consonant *f*; short *i*; consonant *r*; consonant *h*; final /z/ spelled *s*; consonant *b*; consonant *g* (hard); short *o*; consonant *l*; consonant *x*; inflection *-s*; short *e*; consonant *y*; consonant *w*; consonant *k*; consonant *v*; consonant *j*; short *u*; /kw/ spelled *qu*; consonant *z*; double final consonants *ll*; double final consonants *ss*; consonants *-ck*; double final consonants *ff*; double final consonants *zz*; blends with *r*; blends with *l*; blends with *s*

Stan Sleds

DECODABLE WORDS

Target Skill: **blends with *s***

sled	slick	slip	spot	still
sleds	slid	sped	Stan	stuck

Previously Taught Skills

can	hill	it
flat	his	not
has	is	on

SKILLS APPLIED IN WORDS IN STORY: consonants *s, c, t*; short *a*; consonant *n*; consonant *d*; consonant *p*; consonant *f*; short *i*; consonant *h*; final /z/ spelled *s*; short *o*; consonant *l*; inflection *-s*; short *e*; consonant *k*; short *u*; double final consonants *ll*; consonants *-ck*; blends with *l*; blends with *s*

HIGH-FREQUENCY WORDS

a	now
and	the
does	

Houghton Mifflin Harcourt

Stan Sleds

Here is Clem!
Clip, clop, clip, clop.

The drums go click clack.
Click, clack, click, clack.

We are glad, and we clap!
Clap, clap, clap, clap!

We Clap

Fran has a flag.
The flag flaps.
Flap, flap, flap.

High-Frequency Words Taught to Date

Grade 1

a	do	good	I	now	some	why
all	does	have	is	of	the	with
and	every	he	like	our	they	would
animal	find	hear	look	play	to	you
are	for	help	make	pull	today	
away	friend	her	many	said	too	
be	full	here	me	see	we	
call	funny	hold	my	she	what	
come	go	how	no	sing	who	

Decoding skills taught to date: consonants *m, s, c, t*; short *a*; consonant *n*; consonant *d*; consonant *p*; consonant *f*; short *i*; consonant *r*; consonant *h*; /z/ spelled *s*; consonant *b*; consonant *g* (hard); short *o*; consonant *l*; consonant *x*; inflection *-s*; short *e*; consonant *y*; consonant *w*; consonant *k*; consonant *v*; consonant *j*; short *u*; /kw/ spelled *qu*; consonant *z*; final consonants *ll*; final consonants *ss*; consonants *-ck*; final consonants *ff*; final consonants *zz*; blends with *r*; blends with *l*

We Clap

DECODABLE WORDS

Target Skill: **blends with *l***

clack	Clem	clip	flag	flaps
clap	click	clop	flap	glad

Previously Taught Skills

drums	has
Fran	is

SKILLS APPLIED IN WORDS IN STORY: consonants *m, s, c, t*; short *a*; consonant *n*; consonant *d*; consonant *p*; consonant *f*; short *i*; consonant *r*; consonant *h*; /z/ spelled *s*; consonant *g* (hard); short *o*; consonant *l*; inflection *-s*; short *e*; consonant *w*; consonant *k*; short *u*; consonants *-ck*; blends with *r*; blends with *l*

HIGH-FREQUENCY WORDS

a	are	here	we
and	go	the	

Houghton Mifflin Harcourt

blends with *l*

BOOK 62

We Clap

Ducks in the flock quack.
Flap, quack, flap.

Cluck.

Cluck, cluck, cluck.
Ducks can not cluck.
Who said "Cluck"?
A **hen** in the flock clucks!

The flock can quack and flap and cluck.
Quack, flap, cluck!

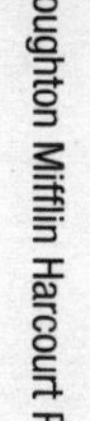

Quack, Flap, Cluck

Ducks in the flock flap.
Flap, flap, flap.

High-Frequency Words Taught to Date

Grade 1

a	come	funny	here	many	pull	to	would
all	do	go	hold	me	said	today	you
and	does	good	how	my	see	too	
animal	every	have	I	no	she	we	
are	find	he	is	now	sing	what	
away	for	hear	like	of	some	who	
be	friend	help	look	our	the	why	
call	full	her	make	play	they	with	

Decoding skills taught to date: consonants *m, s, c, t*; short *a*; consonant *n*; consonant *d*; consonant *p*; consonant *f*; short *i*; consonant *r*; consonant *h*; /z/ spelled *s*; consonant *b*; consonant *g*; short *o*; consonant *l*; consonant *x*; inflection *-s*; short *e*; consonant *y*; consonant *w*; consonant *k*; consonant *v*; consonant *j*; short *u*; /kw/ spelled *qu*; consonant *z*; final consonants *ll*; final consonants *ss*; consonants *ck*; final consonants *ff*; final consonants *zz*; blends with *r*; blends with *l*

Quack, Flap, Cluck

DECODABLE WORDS

Target Skill: **blends with *l***

cluck	flap
clucks	flock

Previously Taught Skills

can	in
ducks	not
hen	quack

SKILLS APPLIED IN WORDS IN STORY: consonants *s, c, t*; short *a*; consonant *n*; consonant *d*; consonant *p*; consonant *f*; short *i*; consonant *h*; short *o*; consonant *l*; consonant *k*; inflection *-s*; short *e*; short *u*; /kw/ spelled *qu*; consonants *-ck*; blends with *l*

HIGH-FREQUENCY WORDS

a	said	who
and	the	

Houghton Mifflin Harcourt

blends with *l*

BOOK 61

Quack, Flap, Cluck

Fred can fill the crack.

Brad grips the drill.
He can drill the rods.

Fran, Fred, and Brad drag the bricks. Fran, Fred, and Brad do a **big** job!

Fran, Fred, and Brad Fix It

Drip, drop, drip, drop. Fran can fix the drip.

High-Frequency Words Taught to Date

Grade 1

a	call	friend	hear	like	of	the	why
all	come	full	help	look	play	they	with
and	do	funny	here	make	pull	to	you
animal	does	go	hold	many	said	too	
are	every	good	how	me	see	we	
away	find	have	I	my	sing	what	
be	for	he	is	no	some	who	

Decoding skills taught to date: consonants *m, s, c, t*; short *a*; consonant *n*; consonant *d*; consonant *p*; consonant *f*; short *i*; consonant *r*; consonant *h*; /z/ spelled *s*; consonant *b*; consonant *g*; short *o*; consonant *l*; consonant *x*; inflection *-s*; short *e*; consonant *y*; consonant *w*; consonant *k*; consonant *v*; consonant *j*; short *u*; /kw/ spelled *qu*; consonant *z*; final consonants *ll*; final consonants *ss*; consonants *ck*; final consonants *ff*; final consonants *zz*; blends with *r*

Fran, Fred, and Brad Fix It

DECODABLE WORDS

Target Skill: **blends with *r***

Brad	drag	drop	grips
bricks	drill	Fran	
crack	drip	Fred	

Previously Taught Skills

big	fill	it	rods
can	fix	job	

SKILLS APPLIED IN WORDS IN STORY: consonants *c, t*; short *a*; consonant *n*; consonant *d*; consonant *p*; consonant *f*; short *i*; consonant *r*; /z/ spelled *s*; consonant *b*; consonant *g* (hard); short *o*; consonant *j*; consonant *x*; inflection *-s*; short *e*; final consonants *ll*; consonants *ck*; blends with *r*

HIGH-FREQUENCY WORDS

a	and	do	he	the

Houghton Mifflin Harcourt.

blends with *r*

BOOK 60

Fran, Fred, and Brad Fix It

Wet drops drip on Gran.
Wet drops drip on the frog.
Gran grabs a hat.

Drip, drop, drip, drop, drip!
Drops drip off the hat brim.
Gran gets wet.

The frog gets wet, too.
It hops in the drops.
Gran grins at the frog.

Drops Drip on Gran

Gran likes animals.
"I see a frog," said Gran.

High-Frequency Words Taught to Date

Grade 1

a	call	friend	hear	like	of	the	why
all	come	full	help	look	play	they	with
and	do	funny	here	make	pull	to	you
animal	does	go	hold	many	said	too	
are	every	good	how	me	see	we	
away	find	have	I	my	sing	what	
be	for	he	is	no	some	who	

Decoding skills taught to date: consonants *m, s, c, t*; short *a*; consonant *n*; consonant *d*; consonant *p*; consonant *f*; short *i*; consonant *r*; consonant *h*; /z/ spelled *s*; consonant *b*; consonant *g* (hard); short *o*; consonant *l*; consonant *x*; inflection *-s*; short *e*; consonant *y*; consonant *w*; consonant *k*; consonant *v*; consonant *j*; short *u*; /kw/ spelled *qu*; consonant *z*; final consonants *ll*; final consonants *ss*; consonants *-ck*; final consonants *ff*; final consonants *zz*; blends with *r*

Drops Drip on Gran

DECODABLE WORDS

Target Skill: **blends with *r***

brim	drops	Gran
drip	frog	grins
drop	grabs	

Previously Taught Skills

at	hat	in	off	wet
gets	hops	it	on	

SKILLS APPLIED IN WORDS IN STORY: consonants *m, t*; short *a*; consonant *n*; consonant *d*; consonant *p*; consonant *f*; short *i*; consonant *r*; consonant *h*; consonant *b*; consonant *g* (hard); short *o*; inflection *-s*; short *e*; consonant *w*; double consonants *ff*; blends with *r*

HIGH-FREQUENCY WORDS

a	likes	the
animals	said	too
I	see	

Houghton Mifflin Harcourt.

blends with *r*

BOOK 59

Drops Drip on Gran

Max runs and runs.
He sees a log.
Max sees his pal Nat.
Max and Nat sit on the log.

They see fuzz. Max picks it up.
Max gets fuzz on Nat!

Max and Nat get off the log.
It is hot, hot, hot!
Max and Nat get pop.
It has fizz. Yum! Yum! Yum!

Max Runs

Here is Max.
Max can run.
He runs up hills.
Max hears a bug buzz.
He looks at it.

High-Frequency Words Taught to Date

Grade 1

a	come	full	help	many	see	what
all	do	funny	here	me	sing	who
and	does	go	hold	my	the	with
are	every	good	I	no	they	you
away	find	have	is	play	to	
be	for	he	like	pull	too	
call	friend	hear	look	said	we	

Decoding skills taught to date: consonants *m, s, t, c*; short *a*; consonant *n*; consonant *d*; consonant *p*; consonant *f*; short *i*; consonant *r*; consonant *h*; /z/ spelled *s*; consonant *b*; consonant *g* (hard); short *o*; consonant *l*; consonant *x*; inflection *-s*; short *e*; consonant *y*; consonant *w*; consonant *k*; consonant *v*; consonant *j*; short *u*; /kw/ spelled *qu*; consonant *z*; final consonants *ll*; final consonants *ss*; consonants *ck*, final consonants *ff*; final consonants *zz*

Max Runs

DECODABLE WORDS

Target Skill: **final consonants *zz***

buzz	fizz	fuzz

Previously Taught Skills

bug	hills	log	pal	sit
can	his	Max	picks	up
get	hot	Nat	pop	yum
gets	is	off	run	
has	it	on	runs	

SKILLS APPLIED IN WORDS IN STORY: consonants *m, s, t, c*; short *a*; consonant *n*; consonant *p*; consonant *f*; short *i*; consonant *r*; consonant *h*; /z/ spelled *s*; consonant *b*; consonant *g* (hard); short *o*; consonant *l*; consonant *x*; inflection *-s*; short *e*; consonant *y*; short *u*; final consonants *ll*; consonants *ck*; final consonants *ff*; final consonants *zz*

HIGH-FREQUENCY WORDS

a	he	here	see	the
and	hears	look(s)	sees	they

Houghton Mifflin Harcourt

final consonants *zz*

BOOK 58

Max Runs

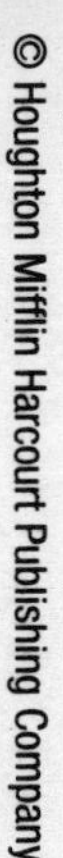

Mom did not see the bug.
It is quick!

The bug is back.
It is big!
It has fuzz, and it can buzz!

Go away, bug!

Mom gets Jazz a cup.
It has fizz.
No bug, no fuzz, no buzz!

Buzz, Fuzz, Fizz

Jazz looks at a bug.
It has fuzz.
It can buzz.

High-Frequency Words Taught to Date

Grade 1

a	come	full	help	many	see	what
all	do	funny	here	me	sing	who
and	does	go	hold	my	the	with
are	every	good	I	no	they	you
away	find	have	is	play	to	
be	for	he	like	pull	too	
call	friend	hear	look	said	we	

Decoding skills taught to date: consonants *m, s, t, c*; short *a*; consonant *n*; consonant *d*; consonant *p*; consonant *f*; short *i*; consonant *r*; consonant *h*; /z/ spelled *s*; consonant *b*; consonant *g* (hard); short *o*; consonant *l*; consonant *x*; inflection *-s*; short *e*; consonant *y*; consonant *w*; consonant *k*; consonant *v*; consonant *j*; short *u*; /kw/ spelled *qu*; consonant *z*; final consonants *ll*; final consonants *ss*; consonants *ck*; final consonants *ff*; final consonants *zz*

Buzz, Fuzz, Fizz

DECODABLE WORDS

Target Skill: **final consonants *zz***

buzz	fizz	fuzz	Jazz

Previously Taught Skills

at	bug	did	is	not
back	can	gets	it	quick
big	cup	has	Mom	

SKILLS APPLIED IN WORDS IN STORY: consonants *m, s, t, c*; short *a*; consonant *n*; consonant *p*; consonant *f*; short *i*; consonant *h*; /z/ spelled *s*; consonant *b*; consonant *g* (hard); short *o*; inflection *-s*; short *e*; consonant *j*; short *u*; /kw/ spelled *qu*; final consonants *zz*; consonants *ck*

HIGH-FREQUENCY WORDS

a	away	looks	see	with
and	go	no	the	

Houghton Mifflin Harcourt

Buzz, Fuzz, Fizz

The muff is off.
Liz is not hot.

A big puff!
Liz can see the muff go up,
up, up, up!

Liz can not find it.
Can you help Liz?

Muff in a Big Puff

Liz has on a muff.
Liz is hot in the muff.

High-Frequency Words Taught to Date

Grade 1

a	call	for	have	I	my	sing	what
all	come	friend	he	is	no	the	who
and	do	full	hear	like	play	they	with
are	does	funny	help	look	pull	to	you
away	every	go	here	many	said	too	
be	find	good	hold	me	see	we	

Decoding skills taught to date: consonants *m, s, t, c*, short *a*; consonant *n*; consonant *d*; consonant *p*; consonant *f*; short *i*; consonant *r*; consonant *h*; /z/ spelled *s*; consonant *b*; consonant *g* (hard); short *o*; consonant *l*; consonant *x*; inflection *-s*; short *e*; consonant *y*; consonant *w*; consonant *k*; consonant *v*; consonant *j*; short *u*; /kw/ spelled *qu*; consonant *z*; final consonants *ll*; final consonants *ss*; consonants *ck*; final consonants *ff*

Muff in a Big Puff

DECODABLE WORDS

Target Skill: **final consonants *ff***

muff	off	puff	

Previously Taught Skills

big	has	is	not
can	hot	it	on
go	in	Liz	up

SKILLS APPLIED IN WORDS IN STORY: consonants: *m, t, c,* short *a*; consonant *n*; consonant *p*; short *i*; consonant *h*; /z/ spelled *s*; consonant *b*; consonant *g* (hard); short *o*; inflection *-s*; consonant *z*; short *u*; consonant *p*; final consonants *ff*

HIGH-FREQUENCY WORDS

a	help	the
find	see	you

Houghton Mifflin Harcourt

final consonants *ff*

BOOK 56

Muff in a Big Puff

Jeff and Ruff go up.
Jeff has to lug a big pack.
Huff, puff.
Huff, puff.

Jeff and Ruff go up, up, up.
Jeff huffs. Jeff puffs.
Ruff huffs. Ruff puffs.
Huff, puff. Huff, puff. Huff, puff.

They did it!
Jeff and Ruff are at the top.
Jeff sits. Ruff sits.
Good job!

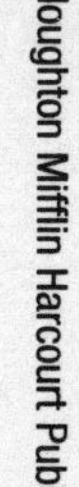

Jeff and Ruff

Jeff will go up a big hill.
His dog, Ruff, will go, too.

High-Frequency Words Taught to Date

Grade 1

a	call	for	have	I	my	sing	what
all	come	friend	he	is	no	the	who
and	do	full	hear	like	play	they	with
are	does	funny	help	look	pull	to	you
away	every	go	here	many	said	too	
be	find	good	hold	me	see	we	

Decoding skills taught to date: consonants *m, s, t, c*, short *a*; consonant *n*; consonant *d*; consonant *p*; consonant *f*; short *i*; consonant *r*; consonant *h*; /z/ spelled *s*; consonant *b*; consonant *g* (hard); short *o*; consonant *l*; consonant *x*; inflection *-s*; short *e*; consonant *y*; consonant *w*; consonant *k*; consonant *v*; consonant *j*; short *u*; /kw/ spelled *qu*; consonant *z*; final consonants *ll*; final consonants *ss*; consonants *ck*; final consonants *ff*

Jeff and Ruff

DECODABLE WORDS

Target Skill: **final consonants *ff***

huff(s)	Jeff	puff(s)	Ruff

Previously Taught Skills

at	dog	his	lug	top
big	has	it	pack	up
did	hill	job	sits	will

SKILLS APPLIED IN WORDS IN STORY: consonants: *s, t,* short *a*; consonant *d*; consonant *p*; short *i*; consonant *r*; consonant *h*; /z/ spelled *s*; consonant *b*; consonant *g* (hard); inflection *-s*; short *e*; short *o*; consonant *l*; consonant *w*; consonant *j*; short *u*; final consonant *ll*; consonants *ck*; final consonant *ff*

HIGH-FREQUENCY WORDS

a	go	they
and	good	to
are	the	too

Houghton Mifflin Harcourt

final consonants *ff*

BOOK 55

Jeff and Ruff

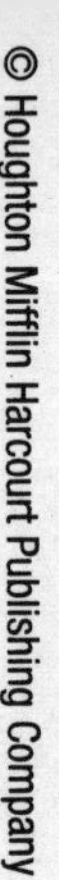

Rick said, "Jack, you
look sad."
Jack Duck said, "Quack.
Quack. Quack."

Rick said, "Get in here,
Jack."
Jack Duck said, "Quack!
Quack!"

"Quack! Quack! Quack!"

Jack Duck

Jack Duck is not well.
He sat on a dock.
He did not get wet.
Jack Duck said, "Quack.
Quack. Quack."

High-Frequency Words Taught to Date

Grade 1

a	call	for	have	I	my	sing	what
all	come	friend	he	is	no	the	who
and	do	full	hear	like	play	they	with
are	does	funny	help	look	pull	to	you
away	every	go	here	many	said	too	
be	find	good	hold	me	see	we	

Decoding skills taught to date: consonants *m, s, c, t*; short *a*; consonant *n*; consonant *d*; consonant *p*; consonant *f*; short *i*; consonant *r*; consonant *h*; /z/ spelled *s*; consonant *b*; consonant *g* (hard); short *o*; consonant *l*; consonant *x*; inflection *-s*; short *e*; consonant *y*; consonant *w*; consonant *k*; consonant *v*; consonant *j*; short *u*; /kw/ spelled *qu*; consonant *z*; final consonants *ll*; final consonants *ss*; consonants *ck*

Jack Duck

DECODABLE WORDS

Target Skill: **consonants *ck***

dock	Jack	Rick
duck	quack	

Previously Taught Skills

can	in	not	sad	well
get	is	on	sat	

SKILLS APPLIED IN WORDS IN STORY: consonants *s, c, t*; short *a*; consonant *n*; consonant *d*; short *i*; consonant *r*; /z/ spelled *s*; short *e*; consonant *w*; consonant *g* (hard); short *o*; consonant *j*; short *u*; /kw/ spelled *qu*; final consonants *ll*; consonants *ck*

HIGH-FREQUENCY WORDS

a	here	said
he	look	you

Houghton Mifflin Harcourt.

consonants *ck*

BOOK 54

Jack Duck

Jack has **his** back pack.
Did Jack pack like Mack?

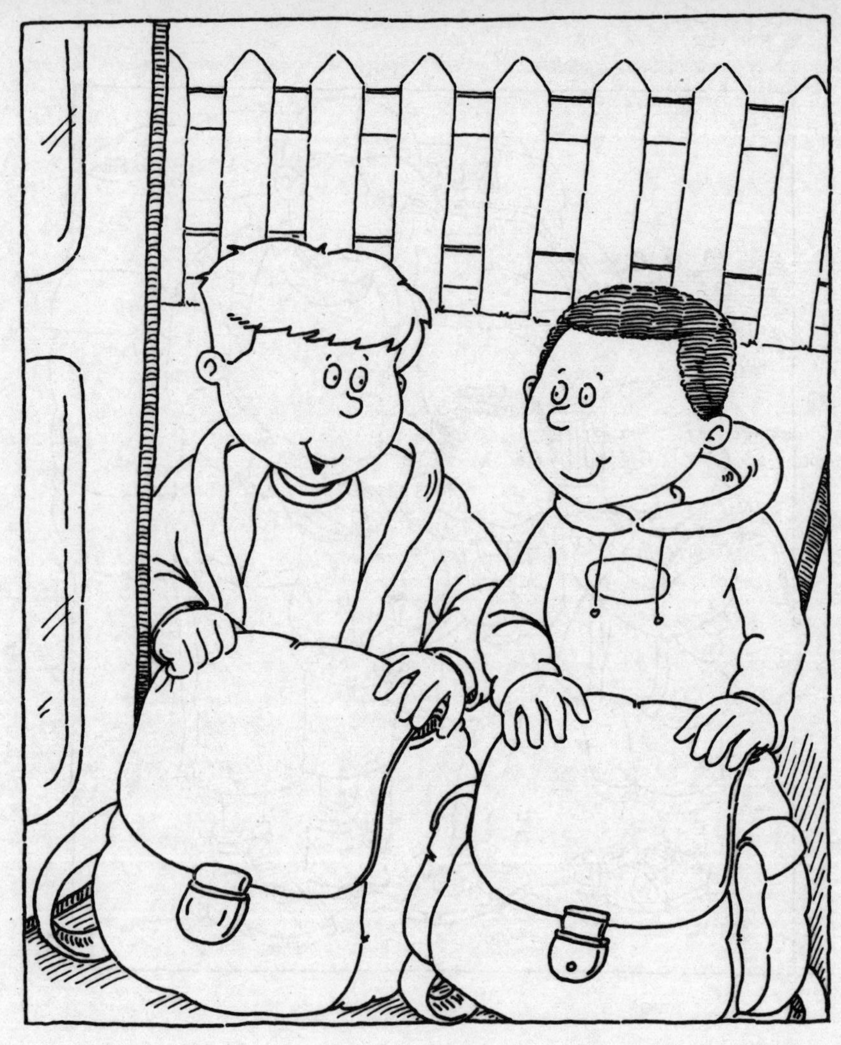

Mack and Jack get on the bus.

Mack and Jack are here!
The pals will have fun.

Back Pack Pals

Mack packs his back pack.
He packs his cap, map,
and socks.

High-Frequency Words Taught to Date

Grade 1

a	call	for	have	I	my	sing	what
all	come	friend	he	is	no	the	who
and	do	full	hear	like	play	they	with
are	does	funny	help	look	pull	to	you
away	every	go	here	many	said	too	
be	find	good	hold	me	see	we	

Decoding skills taught to date: consonants *m, s, t, c*, short a; consonant *n*; consonant *d*; consonant *p*; consonant *f*; short *i*; consonant *r*; consonant *h*; /z/ spelled *s*; consonant *b*; consonant *g* (hard); short *o*; consonant *l*; consonant *x*; inflection *s*; short *e*; consonant y; consonant *w*; consonant *k*; consonant *v*; consonant *j*; short *u*; /kw/ spelled *qu*; consonant *z*; final consonants *ll*; final consonants *ss*; consonants *ck*

Back Pack Pals

DECODABLE WORDS

Target Skill: **consonants *ck***

back Jack Mack pack(s) socks

Previously Taught Skills

bus did has map pals
cap get his on will

SKILLS APPLIED IN WORDS IN STORY: consonants: *m, s, t, c*, short *a*; consonant *n*; consonant *d*; consonant *p*; short *i*; consonant *h*; /z/ spelled *s*; consonant *b*; consonant *g* (hard); short *o*; consonant *l*; short *e*; inflection *-s*; short *u*; consonants *ck*

HIGH-FREQUENCY WORDS

and have here the
are he like

Houghton Mifflin Harcourt

consonants *ck*

BOOK 53

Back Pack Pals

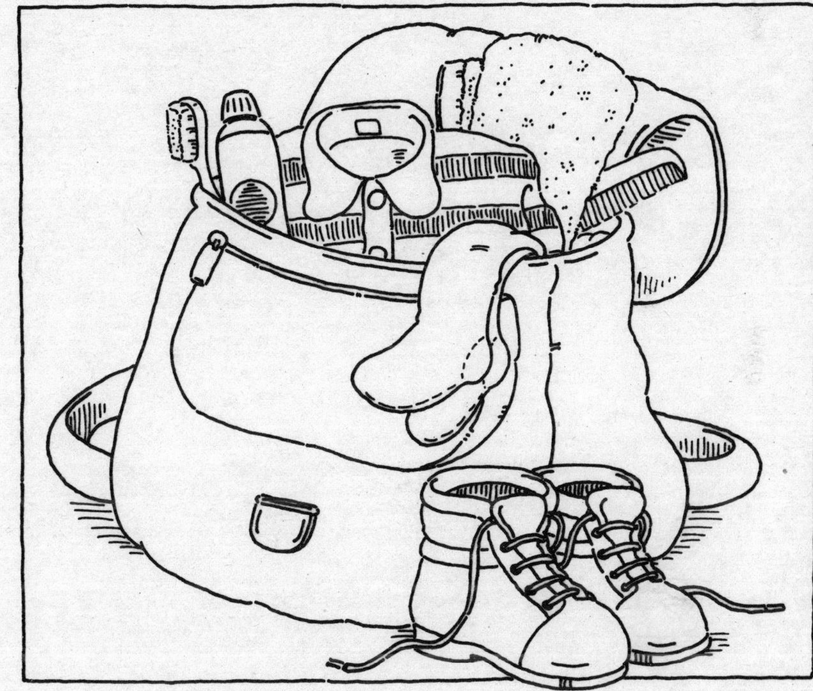

"I can get it, Tess," said Bess.
"Yes, yes, yes, Bess!" said Tess.

Tess can pass Bess the cup.

"It is for you, Mom," said Bess and Tess.
Tess got a kiss.
Bess got a kiss.
Kiss! Kiss! Kiss!

Tess, Bess, and Mom

"I can get it, Bess," said Tess.
"Yes, yes, yes, Tess!" said Bess.

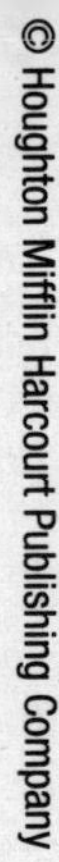

High-Frequency Words Taught to Date

Grade 1

a	come	full	help	many	see	what
all	do	funny	here	me	sing	who
and	does	go	hold	my	the	with
are	every	good	I	no	they	you
away	find	have	is	play	to	
be	for	he	like	pull	too	
call	friend	hear	look	said	we	

Decoding skills taught to date: consonants *m, s, t, c*; short *a*; consonant *n*; consonant *d*; consonant *p*; consonant *f*; short *i*; consonant *r*; consonant *h*; /z/ spelled *s*; consonant *b*; consonant *g* (hard); short *o*; consonant *l*; consonant *x*; inflection *-s*; short *e*; consonant *y*; consonant *w*; consonant *k*; consonant *v*; consonant *j*; short *u*; /kw/ spelled *qu*; consonant *z*; final consonants *ll*; final consonants *ss*

Tess, Bess, and Mom

DECODABLE WORDS

Target Skill: **final consonants *ss***

Bess	kiss	pass	Tess

Previously Taught Skills

can	get	is	Mom
cup	got	it	yes

SKILLS APPLIED IN WORDS IN STORY: consonants *m, s, t, c*; short *a*; consonant *n*; consonant *p*; short *i*; /z/ spelled *s*; consonant *b*; consonant *g* (hard); short *o*; short *e*; consonant *y*; consonant *k*; short *u*; final consonants *ss*

HIGH-FREQUENCY WORDS

a	for	said
and	I	you

Houghton Mifflin Harcourt

Tess, Bess, and Mom

A bass is up.
Jess has a net.

Will Jess get a bass?
Will the bass pass his net?

Jess did not get a bass.
But he had fun!

Will Jess Get a Bass?

Here are bass.

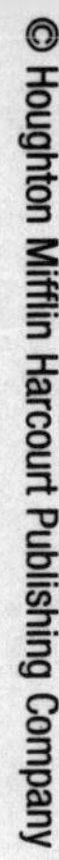

High-Frequency Words Taught to Date

Grade 1

a	come	full	help	many	see	what
all	do	funny	here	me	sing	who
and	does	go	hold	my	the	with
are	every	good	I	no	they	you
away	find	have	is	play	to	
be	for	he	like	pull	too	
call	friend	hear	look	said	we	

Decoding skills taught to date: consonants *m, s, t, c*; short *a*; consonant *n*; consonant *d*; consonant *p*; consonant *f*; short *i*; consonant *r*; consonant *h*; /z/ spelled *s*; consonant *b*; consonant *g* (hard); short *o*; consonant *l*; consonant *x*; inflection *-s*; short *e*; consonant *y*; consonant *w*; consonant *k*; consonant *v*; consonant *j*; short *u*; /kw/ spelled *qu*; consonant *z*; final consonants *ll*; final consonants *ss*

Will Jess Get a Bass?

DECODABLE WORDS

Target Skill: **final consonants *ss***

bass	Jess	pass

Previously Taught Skills

but	get	his	not
did	had	is	up
fun	has	net	will

SKILLS APPLIED IN WORDS IN STORY: consonants *s, t, c*; short *a*; consonant *n*; consonant *d*; consonant *f*; consonant *p*; short *i*; consonant *h*; /z/ spelled *s*; consonant *b*; consonant *g* (hard); short *o*; short *e*; consonant *w*; consonant *j*; short *u*; final consonants *ll*; final consonants *ss*

HIGH-FREQUENCY WORDS

a	he	see
are	here	the

Houghton Mifflin Harcourt

final consonants *ss*

BOOK 51

Will Jess Get a Bass?

Bill is a fun dog.
Jill tells Bill to go get it!

Bill and Jill run a lot.
Bill and Jill get hot, hot, hot.

Jill can fill a pan for Bill.
Jill can fill a cup, too.

Bill and Jill

Jill runs on a hill.
Bill runs on a hill, too!

High-Frequency Words Taught to Date

Grade 1

a	call	for	have	I	my	sing	what
all	come	friend	he	is	no	the	who
and	do	full	hear	like	play	they	with
are	does	funny	help	look	pull	to	you
away	every	go	here	many	said	too	
be	find	good	hold	me	see	we	

Decoding skills taught to date: consonants *m, s, t, c*; short *a*; consonant *n*; consonant *d*; consonant *p*; consonant *f*; short *i*; consonant *r*; consonant *h*; consonant *s* /z/; consonant *b*; hard *g*; short *o*; consonant *l*; consonant *x*; inflection *-s*; short *e*; consonant *y*; consonant *w*; consonant *k*; consonant *v*; consonant *j*; short *u*; consonants *qu*; consonant *z*; double final consonants *ll*

Bill and Jill

DECODABLE WORDS

Target Skill: **final consonants: *ll***

Bill	fill	hill	Jill	tells

Previously Taught Skills

can	fun	is	pan	yes
cup	get	it	run	
dog	hot	on	runs	

SKILLS APPLIED IN WORDS IN STORY: consonants *s, t, c*; short *a*; consonant *n*; consonant *d*; consonant *p*; consonant *f*; short *i*; consonant *r*; consonant *h*; consonant *s* /*z*/; consonant *b*; consonant *g* (hard); short *o*; consonant *l*; consonant *y*; consonant *j*; short *u*; double final consonants *ll*

HIGH-FREQUENCY WORDS

a	for	plays	too
and	go	to	

Houghton Mifflin Harcourt

Bill and Jill

Lill set Bell Doll on a sill.

Bell Doll fell.

Lill tells Bell Doll to get well.

Lill will help!

Lill sets Bell Doll in bed.
Bell Doll will get well.

Get Well, Bell Doll

Lill has a doll.
The doll is Bell.

High-Frequency Words Taught to Date

Grade 1

a	call	for	have	I	my	sing	what
all	come	friend	he	is	no	the	who
and	do	full	hear	like	play	they	with
are	does	funny	help	look	pull	to	you
away	every	go	here	many	said	too	
be	find	good	hold	me	see	we	

Decoding skills taught to date: consonants *m, s, t, c*; short *a*; consonant *n*; consonant *d*; consonant *p*; consonant *f*; short *i*; consonant *r*; consonant *h*; consonant *s* /z/; consonant *b*; hard *g*; short *o*; consonant *l*; consonant *x*; inflection *-s*; short *e*; consonant *y*; consonant *w*; consonant *k*; consonant *v*; consonant *j*; short *u*; consonants *qu*; consonant *z*; double final consonants *ll*

Get Well, Bell Doll

DECODABLE WORDS

Target Skill: **final consonants *ll***

Bell	fell	sill	well
Doll	Lill	tells	will

Previously Taught Skills

bed	has	on	sets
get	is	set	

SKILLS APPLIED IN WORDS IN STORY: consonants *s, t*; short *a*; consonant *d*; consonant *f*; short *i*; consonant *h*; consonant *s* /z/; consonant *b*; hard *g*; short *o*; consonant *l*; inflection *-s*; short *e*; consonant *w*; short *u*; double final consonants *ll*

HIGH-FREQUENCY WORDS

a	help	the	to

Houghton Mifflin Harcourt

final consonants *ll*

BOOK 49

Get Well, Bell Doll

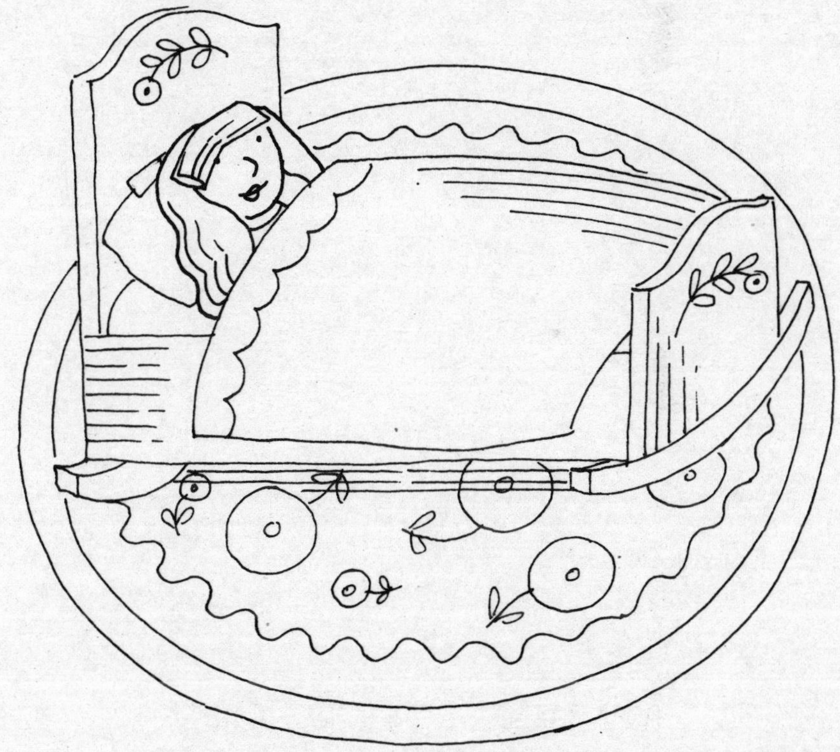

My bag zips up. Zip!

My top zips up. Zip!

Zip! Zip! Zip!

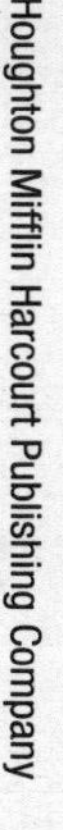

Zip, Zip, Zip

My kit zips up. Zip!

High-Frequency Words Taught to Date

Grade 1

a	do	full	he	is	my	sing	we
all	does	funny	help	like	no	the	what
and	find	go	here	look	play	they	who
are	for	good	hold	many	pull	to	with
be	friend	have	I	me	see	too	you

Decoding skills taught to date: consonants *m, s, c, t*; short *a*; consonant *n*; consonant *d*; consonant *p*; consonant *f*; short *i*; consonant *r*; consonant *h*; final /z/ spelled *s*; consonant *b*; consonant *g* (hard); short *o*; consonant *l*; consonant *x*; inflection *-s*; short *e*; consonant *y*; consonant *w*; consonant *k*; consonant *v*; consonant *j*; short *u*; /kw/ spelled *qu*; consonant *z*

Zip, Zip, Zip

DECODABLE WORDS

Target Skill: **consonant *z***

zip

zips

Previously Taught Skills

bag
top
kit
up

SKILLS APPLIED IN WORDS IN STORY: consonants *s, t*; short *a*; consonant *p*; short *i*; consonant *b*; consonant *g* (hard); short *o*; inflection *-s*; consonant *k*; short *u*; consonant *z*

HIGH-FREQUENCY WORDS

my

Houghton Mifflin Harcourt

consonant *z*

BOOK 48

Zip, Zip, Zip

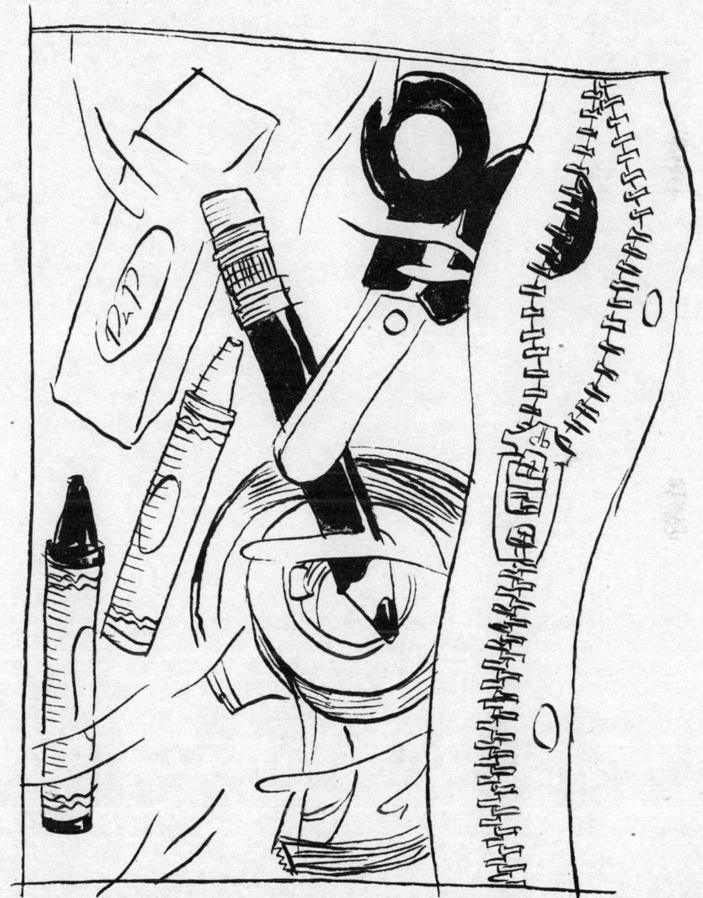

I zag!

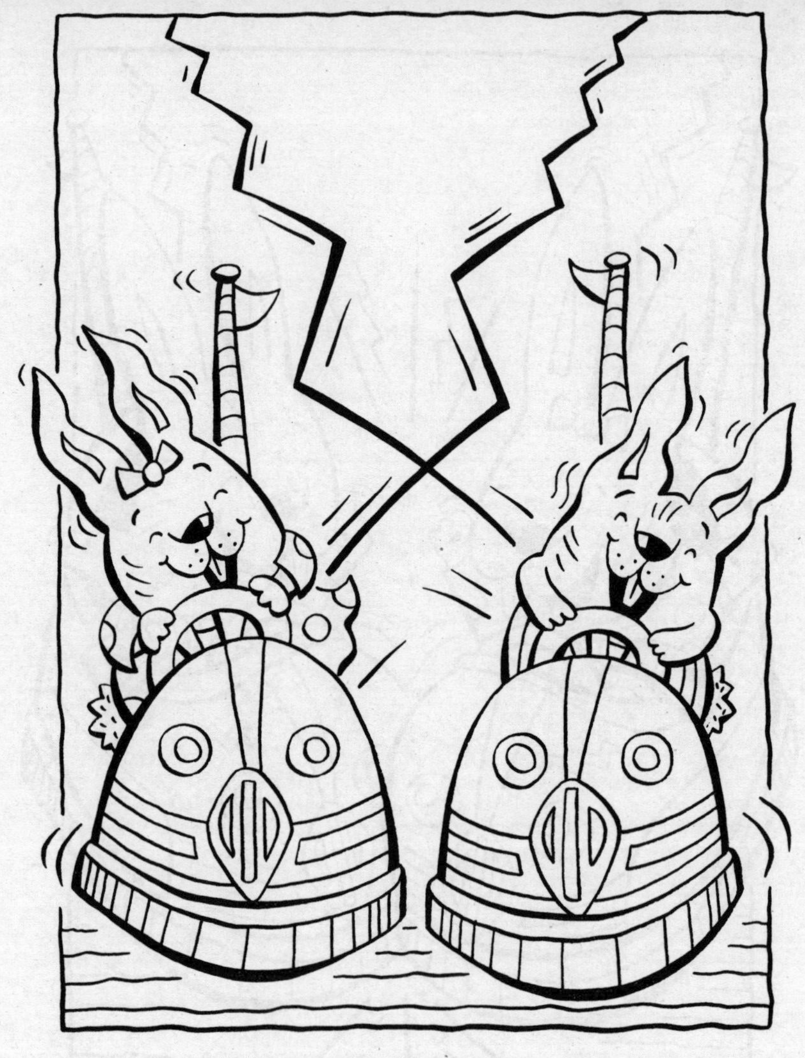

I zig. I zag.
Zig-zag. Zig-zag.

Zig, zag, zap!

consonant *z*

BOOK 47

The Big Zig-Zag

I zig!

High-Frequency Words Taught to Date

Grade 1

a	do	full	he	is	my	sing	we
all	does	funny	help	like	no	the	what
and	find	go	here	look	play	they	who
are	for	good	hold	many	pull	to	with
be	friend	have	I	me	see	too	you

Decoding skills taught to date: consonants *m, s, t, c*; short *a*; consonant *n*; consonant *d*; consonant *p*; consonant *f*; short *i*; consonant *r*; consonant *h*; consonant *s* /z/; consonant *b*; consonant *g* (hard); short *o*; consonant *l*; consonant *x*; inflection *–s*; short *e*; consonant *y*; consonant *w*; consonant *k*; consonant *v*; consonant *j*; short *u*; consonant *q(u)*; consonant *z*

The Big Zig-Zag

DECODABLE WORDS

Target Skill: **consonant *z***

zag zap zig zig-zag

Previously Taught Skills

big

SKILLS APPLIED IN WORDS IN STORY: short *a*; consonant *p*; short *i*; consonant *b*; consonant *g* (hard); consonant *z*

HIGH-FREQUENCY WORDS

I the

Houghton Mifflin Harcourt.

consonant *z*

BOOK 47

The Big Zig-Zag

Quig had a nut.
Quig had a lot!

Quig had a big bun with jam.
Quig had ten!

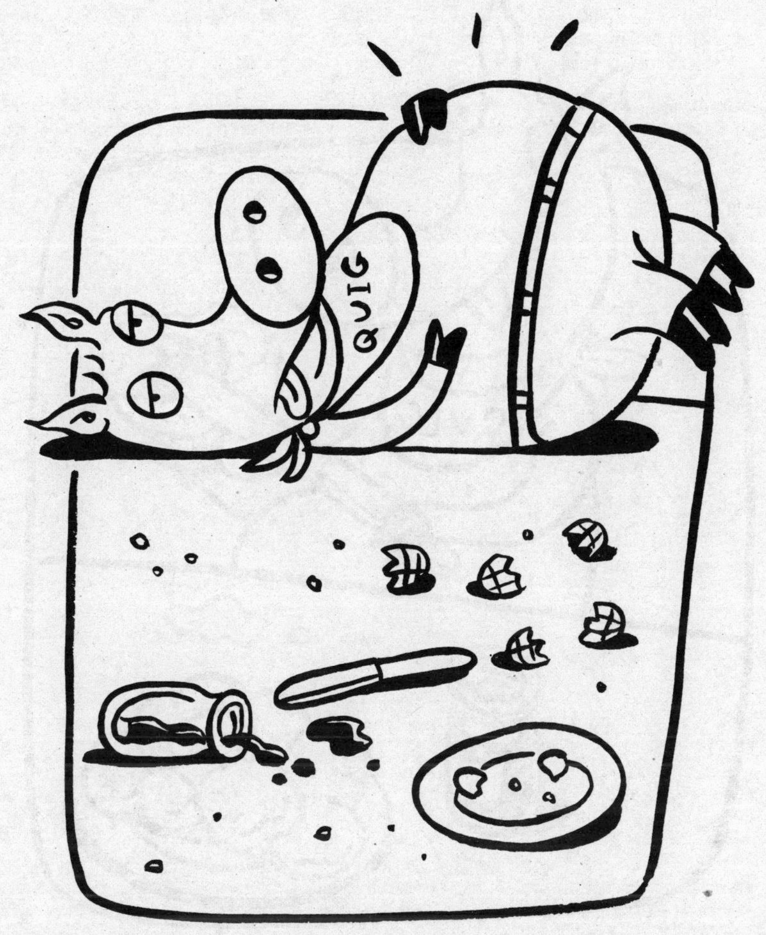

Quig did not get up.
Quig quit.

Quig Pig!

Quig had a fig.
Quig had six!

High-Frequency Words Taught to Date

Grade 1

a	do	full	he	is	my	sing	we
all	does	funny	help	like	no	the	with
and	find	go	here	look	play	they	what
are	for	good	hold	many	pull	to	who
be	friend	have	I	me	see	too	you

Decoding skills taught to date: consonants *m, s, t, c*, short *a*; consonant *n*; consonant *d*; consonant *p*; consonant *f*, short *i*; consonant *r*; consonant *h*; consonant *s /z/*; consonant *b*; consonant *g* (hard); short *o*; consonant *l*; consonant *x*; inflection *-s*; short *e*; consonant *y*; consonant *w*; consonant *k*; consonant *v*; consonant *j*; short *u*; consonant *q(u)*

Quig Pig!

DECODABLE WORDS

Target Skill: **consonant *q(u)***

Quig	quit

Previously Taught Skills

big	get	lot	six
bun	had	not	ten
fig	jam	nut	up

SKILLS APPLIED IN WORDS IN STORY: consonants *m, s, t, c*, short *a*; consonant *n*; consonant *d*; consonant *p*; consonant *f*; short *i*; consonant *h*; consonant *b*; consonant *g* (hard); short *o*; consonant *l*; consonant *x*; short *e*; consonant *j*; short *u*; consonant *q(u)*

HIGH-FREQUENCY WORDS

a	with

Houghton Mifflin Harcourt

consonant *q(u)*

BOOK 46

Quig Pig!

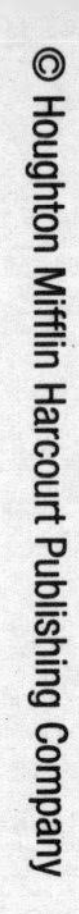

Quin did not get a hit.
But Quin did not quit.

Quin ran.
Tim ran.
Quon ran.
Who wins?

Quin wins!
Quin did not quit.

Did Quin Quit?

Quin did not win.
But Quin did not quit.

High-Frequency Words Taught to Date

Grade 1

a	do	full	he	is	my	sing	we
all	does	funny	help	like	no	the	what
and	find	go	here	look	play	they	who
are	for	good	hold	many	pull	to	with
be	friend	have	I	me	see	too	you

Decoding skills taught to date: *m, s, t, c*, short *a*; consonant *n*; consonant *d*; consonant *p*; consonant *f*; short *i*; consonant *r*; consonant *h*; consonant *s* /z/; consonant *b*; consonant *g* (hard); short *o*; consonant *l*; consonant *x*; inflection *–s*; short *e*; consonant *y*; consonant *w*; consonant *k*; consonant *v*; consonant *j*; short *u*; consonant *q(u)*

Did Quin Quit?

DECODABLE WORDS

Target Skill: **consonant *q(u)***

Quin quit Quon

Previously Taught Skills

but get not Tim wins
did hit ran win

SKILLS APPLIED IN WORDS IN STORY: consonant *t*, short *a*; consonant *n*; consonant *d*; short *i*; consonant *r*; consonant *h*; consonant *s*/z/; consonant *b*; consonant *g* (hard); short *o*; inflection –*s*; short *e*; consonant *w*; short *u*

HIGH-FREQUENCY WORDS

a who

Houghton Mifflin Harcourt.

consonant *q(u)*

BOOK 45

Did Quin Quit?

Pup can tug.
Cub can tug.
Pup and Cub have fun!

Pup can hop.
Cub can hop.
Pup and Cub have fun!

Pup hugs Cub.
Cub hugs Pup.

Pup and Cub Have Fun

Pup can run.
Cub can run.
Pup and Cub have fun!

High-Frequency Words Taught to Date

Grade 1

a	do	full	he	is	my	sing	we
all	does	funny	help	like	no	the	what
and	find	go	here	look	play	they	who
are	for	good	hold	many	pull	to	with
be	friend	have	I	me	see	too	you

Decoding skills taught to date: *m, s, t, c*; short *a*; consonant *n*; consonant *d*; consonant *p*; consonant *f*; short *i*; consonant *r*; consonant *h*; consonant *s* /z/; consonant *b*; consonant *g* (hard); short *o*; consonant *l*; consonant *x*; inflection *–s*; short *e*; consonant *y*; consonant *w*; consonant *k*; consonant *v*; consonant *j*; short *u*

Pup and Cub Have Fun

DECODABLE WORDS

Target Skill: **short *u***

Cub	hugs	run
fun	Pup	tug

Previously Taught Skills

can	hop

SKILLS APPLIED IN WORDS IN STORY: consonant *t*; consonant *c*; short *a*; consonant *n*; consonant *p*; consonant *f*; consonant *r*; consonant *h*; consonant *b*; consonant *g* (hard); short *o*; inflection –*s*; short *u*

HIGH-FREQUENCY WORDS

and	have

Houghton Mifflin Harcourt.

short *u*

BOOK 44

Pup and Cub Have Fun

Cub has a cup.
Mom has a mug.

Mom sits in the sun.
Mom cuts the bun.

Yum! Yum! Yum!

Yum! Yum!

Mom and Cub have fun.
They run, run, run.

High-Frequency Words Taught to Date

Grade 1

a	do	full	he	is	my	sing	we
all	does	funny	help	like	no	the	what
and	find	go	here	look	play	they	who
are	for	good	hold	many	pull	to	with
be	friend	have	I	me	see	too	you

Decoding skills taught to date: consonants *m, s, c, t*; short *a*; consonant *n*; consonant *d*; consonant *p*; consonant *f*; short *i*; consonant *r*; consonant *h*; final /z/ spelled *s*; consonant *b*; consonant *g* (hard); short *o*; consonant *l*; consonant *x*; inflection *-s*; short *e*; consonant *y*; consonant *w*; consonant *k*; consonant *v*; consonant *j*; short *u*

Yum! Yum!

DECODABLE WORDS

Target Skill: ***short u***

bun	cup	fun	run	yum
Cub	cuts	mug	sun	

Previously Taught Skills

has	is	Mom
in	it	sits

SKILLS APPLIED IN WORDS IN STORY: consonants *m, s, c, t*; short *a*; consonant *n*; consonant *p*; consonant *f*; short *i*; consonant *r*; consonant *h*; final /z/ spelled *s*; consonant *b*; consonant *g* (hard); short *o*; consonant *y*; short *u*

HIGH-FREQUENCY WORDS

a	have	they
and	the	

Houghton Mifflin Harcourt

short *u*

BOOK 43

Yum! Yum!

Jan gets the hot pan.
Jan has a hot job.

Jed gets the big box.
Jed has a big job.

Jen gets the jet set.
See Jen go.

A Big Job

Jon gets the wet net.
Jon has a wet job.

High-Frequency Words Taught to Date

Grade 1

a	do	go	I	my	the	what
all	does	have	is	no	they	who
and	find	he	like	play	to	with
are	for	help	look	see	too	you
be	funny	here	me	sing	we	

Decoding skills taught to date: consonants *m, s, t, c*; short *a*; consonant *n*; consonant *d*; consonant *p*; consonant *f*; short *i*; consonant *r*; consonant *h*; consonant *s* /z/, consonant *b*; consonant *g* (hard); short *o*; consonant *l*; consonant *x*; inflection *-s*; short *e*; consonant *y*; consonant *w*; consonant *k*; consonant *v*; consonant *j*

A Big Job

DECODABLE WORDS

Target Skill: **consonant *j***

Jan	Jen	job
Jed	jet	Jon

Previously Taught Skills

big	gets	hot	pan	wet
box	has	net	set	

SKILLS APPLIED IN WORDS IN STORY: consonants *s, t, c*; short *a*; consonant *n*; consonant *p*; short *i*; consonant *h*; consonant *s* /z/; consonant *b*; consonant *g* (hard); short *o*; consonant *x*; inflection –*s*; short *e*; consonant *w*; consonant *j*

HIGH-FREQUENCY WORDS

a	go	see	the

Houghton Mifflin Harcourt

consonant *j*

BOOK 42

A Big Job

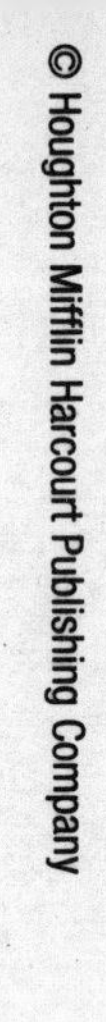

Jim and Jan tap.
They tap, tap, tap in top hats.

Jim bops. Jan hops.
They hop, hop, hop and bop.

Jim and Jan get jam.
Jim and Jan like jam a lot.

Jim and Jan Jig

Jim and Jan jig.
Jim jigs with Jan.
Jan jigs with Jim.

High-Frequency Words Taught to Date

Grade 1

a	do	go	I	my	the	what
all	does	have	is	no	they	who
and	find	he	like	play	to	with
are	for	help	look	see	too	you
be	funny	here	me	sing	we	

Decoding skills taught to date: consonants *m, s, t, c*; short *a*; consonant *n*; consonant *d*; consonant *p*; consonant *f*; short *i*; consonant *r*; consonant *h*; consonant */z/*; consonant *b*; consonant *g* (hard); short *o*; consonant *l*; consonant *x*; inflection *-s*; short *e*; consonant *y*; consonant *w*; consonant *k*; consonant *v*; consonant *j*

Jim and Jan Jig

DECODABLE WORDS

Target Skill: **consonant *j***

jam	Jan	jig	jigs	Jim

Previously Taught Skills

bop	get	hop	in	tap
bops	hats	hops	lot	top

SKILLS APPLIED IN WORDS IN STORY: consonants *m, s, t*; short *a*; consonant *n*, consonant *d*, consonant *p*, consonant *f*; short *i*; consonant *h*, consonant *s* /z/, consonant *b*, consonant *g* (hard); short *o*; consonant *l*; inflection *-s*; short *e*; consonant *j*

HIGH-FREQUENCY WORDS

a	and	do	like	they	with

Houghton Mifflin Harcourt.

consonant *j*

BOOK 41

Jim and Jan Jig

Val, Val, Val,
get in the van!

Val, Val, Val,
do not get wet!

Val, Val, Val,
go to the vet.

consonant *v*

BOOK 40

Val, Val, Val

Val, Val, Val,
get to the pan.

High-Frequency Words Taught to Date

Grade 1

a	do	go	I	my	the	what
all	does	have	is	no	they	who
and	find	he	like	play	to	with
are	for	help	look	see	too	you
be	funny	here	me	sing	we	

Decoding skills taught to date: consonants *m, s, t, c*; short *a*; consonant *n*; consonant *d*; consonant *p*; consonant *f*; short *i*; consonant *r*; consonant *h*; consonant *s/z/*; consonant *b*; consonant *g* (hard); short *o*; consonant *l*; consonant *x*, inflection *-s*; short *e*; consonant *y*; consonant *w*; consonant *k*; consonant *v*

Val, Val, Val

DECODABLE WORDS

Target Skill: **consonant *v***

Val	van	vet

Previously Taught Skills

get	not	wet
in	pan	

SKILLS APPLIED IN WORDS IN STORY: consonant *t*; short *a*; consonant *n;* consonant *p;* short *i*; consonant *g* (hard); short *o*; short *e*; consonant *w*; consonant *v*

HIGH-FREQUENCY WORDS

do	go	the	to

Houghton Mifflin Harcourt.

consonant *v*

BOOK 40

Val, Val, Val

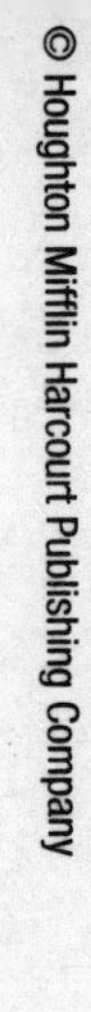

Vic can see the big box.
Can Vic have the big box?
Is it for him?

The tag has "Vic" on it.
Vic gets the big box.

Vic got a big, big van!
"Vvvvrrrr! Look at my big van!"

Viv and Vic

Viv has a big van.
Viv has a big box in the van.
Viv gets the box.

High-Frequency Words Taught to Date

Grade 1

a	do	go	I	my	the	what
all	does	have	is	no	they	who
and	find	he	like	play	to	with
are	for	help	look	see	too	you
be	funny	here	me	sing	we	

Decoding skills taught to date: consonants *m, s, t,* c; short *a*; consonant *n*; consonant *d*; consonant *p*; consonant *f*; short *i*; consonant *r*; consonant *h*; consonant *s* /z/; consonant *b*; consonant *g* (hard); short *o*; consonant *l*; consonant *x*; inflection *–s*; short *e*; consonant *y*; consonant *w*; consonant *k*; consonant *v*

Viv and Vic

DECODABLE WORDS

Target Skill: **consonant *v***

van	Vic	Viv	Vvvvrrrr

Previously Taught Skills

at	can	has	is	tag
big	gets	him	it	
box	got	in	on	

SKILLS APPLIED IN WORDS IN STORY: consonants *m, s, t, c*; short *a*; consonant *n*; short *i*; consonant *h*; consonant *s* /z/; consonant *b*; consonant *g* (hard); short *o*; consonant *x*, inflection *-s*; short *e*; consonant *v*

HIGH-FREQUENCY WORDS

a	for	look	see
and	have	my	the

Houghton Mifflin Harcourt

consonant *v*

BOOK 39

Viv and Vic

The kid nips at Yak.
Ken looks at the kid.
"Kid, kid! It is bad to nip.
Do not nip at Yak!"

The kid nips at Ken.
"Kid! Kid! Do not nip my leg!
It is bad to nip."

Ken fed the kid.
The kid did not nip Yak.
The kid did not nip Ken.

Kid, Kid!

Here is Ken.
Here is a kid.

High-Frequency Words Taught to Date

Grade 1

a	do	go	I	my	the	with
all	does	have	is	no	they	what
and	find	he	like	play	to	who
are	for	help	look	see	too	you
be	funny	here	me	sing	we	

Decoding skills taught to date: consonants *m, s, t,* c; short *a*; consonant *n*; consonant *d*; consonant *p*; consonant *f*; short *i*; consonant *r*; consonant *h*; consonant *s* /*z*/; consonant *b*; consonant *g* (hard); short *o*; consonant *l*; consonant *x*; inflection *–s*; short *e*; consonant *y*; consonant *w*; consonant *k*

Kid, Kid!

DECODABLE WORDS

Target Skill: **consonant *k***

Ken	kid	Yak

Previously Taught Skills

at	fed	leg	not
bad	is	nip	
did	it	nips	

SKILLS APPLIED IN WORDS IN STORY: consonants *s, t;* short *a*; consonant *n*; consonant *d*; consonant *p*; consonant *f*; short *i*; consonant *s* /z/; consonant *b*; consonant *g* (hard); short *o*; inflection *–s;* short *e*; consonant *y*; consonant *k*

HIGH-FREQUENCY WORDS

a	here	my	to
do	looks	the	

Houghton Mifflin Harcourt

Kid, Kid!

Is Kip Cat here?

"Kip! Kip!"

Kim can not find Kip Cat.

Kip Cat is not here.

Kip got the Kip Cat Kit.

"Here, Kip! I got the Kip Cat Kit.

We can play."

Kip Cat does like to play.
Kip Cat ran to Kim.
"Kip! Here is Kip Cat!"

Kim and Kip

Kim can not find Kip Cat.
"Kip! Kip! Kip!"
Kim can not get Kip Cat.

High-Frequency Words Taught to Date

Grade 1

a	do	go	I	my	the	with
all	does	have	is	no	they	what
and	find	he	like	play	to	who
are	for	help	look	see	too	you
be	funny	here	me	sing	we	

Decoding skills taught to date: consonants *m, s, t,* c; short *a*; consonant *n*; consonant *d*; consonant *p*; consonant *f*; short *i*; consonant *r*; consonant *h*; consonant *s /z/*; consonant *b*; consonant *g* (hard); short *o*; consonant *l*; consonant *x*; inflection *–s*; short *e*; consonant *y*; consonant *w*; consonant *k*

Kim and Kip

DECODABLE WORDS

Target Skill: **consonant *k***

Kim	Kip	kit

Previously Taught Skills

can	get	is	ran
Cat	got	not	

SKILLS APPLIED IN WORDS IN STORY: consonants *m, t, c*; short *a*; consonant *p*; consonant *n*; short *i*; consonant *r*; consonant *s* /z/; consonant *g* (hard); short *o*; inflection *–s*; consonant *k*

HIGH-FREQUENCY WORDS

and	find	I	play	to
does	here	like	the	we

Houghton Mifflin Harcourt

consonant *k*

BOOK 37

Kim and Kip

We pin the wig.
We wax the wig.
We can not fix the wig.

Wa! Wa!
Wag Pig is sad.
Wag Pig hid the wig.

Wag Pig got a big hat.
Wag Pig is at the Pig Hop!

Wag Pig and the Wig

Wag Pig has a wig.
It is a bad wig.
Wag Pig can not go
to the Pig Hop.

High-Frequency Words Taught to Date

Grade 1

a	do	go	I	my	the	with
all	does	have	is	no	they	what
and	find	he	like	play	to	who
are	for	help	look	see	too	you
be	funny	here	me	sing	we	

Decoding skills taught to date: consonants *m, s, t,* c; short *a*; consonant *n*; consonant *d*; consonant *p*; consonant *f*; short *i*; consonant *r*; consonant *h*; consonant *s* /z/; consonant *b*,; consonant *g* (hard); short *o*; consonant *l*; consonant *x*; inflection *–s*; short *e*; consonant *y*; consonant *w*

Wag Pig and the Wig

DECODABLE WORDS

Target Skill: **consonant *w***

wa	Wag	wax	wig

Previously Taught Skills

at	fix	hid	not
bad	got	Hop	Pig
big	has	is	pin
can	hat	it	sad

SKILLS APPLIED IN WORDS IN STORY: consonants *s, t, c*; short *a*; consonant *n*; consonant *d*; consonant *p*; consonant *f*; short *i*; consonant *h*; consonant *s* /z/; consonant *g* (hard); short *o*; consonant *x*; consonant *w*

HIGH-FREQUENCY WORDS

a	go	the	to	we
and				

Houghton Mifflin Harcourt

consonant *w*

BOOK 36

Wag Pig and the Wig

Wix taps his bat.

Wix gets a hit!
It is a big, big, big hit!

We win! We win!
Wag, wag, wag.

Can Wix Win It?

We wag, wag, wag.

High-Frequency Words Taught to Date

Grade 1

a	do	go	I	my	the	with
all	does	have	is	no	they	what
and	find	he	like	play	to	who
are	for	help	look	see	too	you
be	funny	here	me	sing	we	

Decoding skills taught to date: consonants *m, s, t,* c; short *a*; consonant *n*; consonant *d*; consonant *p*; consonant *f*; short *i*; consonant *r*; consonant *h*; consonant *s /z/*; consonant *b*; consonant *g* (hard); short *o*; consonant *l*; consonant *x*; inflection *–s*; short *e*; consonant *y*; consonant *w*

Can Wix Win It?

DECODABLE WORDS

Target Skill: **consonant *w***

wag	win	Wix

Previously Taught Skills

bat	gets	hit	it	tag
big	got	hop	not	taps
can	his	is		

SKILLS APPLIED IN WORDS IN STORY: consonants *s, t, c*; short *a*; consonant *n*; consonant *p*; short *i*; consonant *h*; consonant *s/z/*; consonant *b*; consonant *g* (hard); short *o*; consonant *x*; inflection *–s*; short *e*; consonant *w*

HIGH-FREQUENCY WORDS

a	we

Houghton Mifflin Harcourt.

Can Wix Win It?

Yan, can you help me yet?

Not yet, Lin.

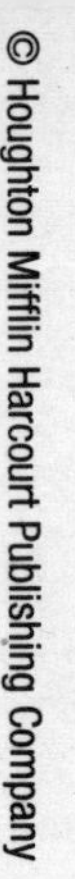

Yan, can you tag me yet?

Yes, Lin. I can!

Yes! Yan can help Lin.

Yes! Lin can hit.

Not Yet

Yan, can you hit yet?

Not yet, Lin.

High-Frequency Words Taught to Date

Grade 1

a	do	go	I	my	the	with
all	does	have	is	no	they	what
and	find	he	like	play	to	who
are	for	help	look	see	too	you
be	funny	here	me	sing	we	

Decoding skills taught to date: consonants *m, s, t,* c; short *a*; consonant *n*; consonant *d*; consonant *p*; consonant *f*; short *i*; consonant *r*; consonant *h*; consonant *s* /z/; consonant *b*; consonant *g* (hard); short *o*; consonant *l*; consonant *x*; inflection *–s*; short *e*; consonant *y*

Not Yet

DECODABLE WORDS

Target Skill: **consonant *y***

Yan yes yet

Previously Taught Skills

can Lin tag
hit not

SKILLS APPLIED IN WORDS IN STORY: consonants *s, t, c*; short *a*; consonant *n*; short *i*; consonant *h*; consonant *g* (hard); short *o*; consonant *l*; short *e*; consonant *y*

HIGH-FREQUENCY WORDS

I help me you

Houghton Mifflin Harcourt

Not Yet

Dad can fit the yams in
a big pan.
Mom helps.

Can Mom mix the yams?
Yes, Mom can.
It is hot, hot, hot!

Do Dad, Mom, and Yan
like yams? Yes! Yes!
They like yams! Mmmm!

Six Yams

Dad, Mom, and Yan have
six big yams.
They can fix the yams.

High-Frequency Words Taught to Date

Grade 1

a	do	go	I	my	the	what
all	does	have	is	no	they	who
and	find	he	like	play	to	with
are	for	help	look	see	too	you
be	funny	here	me	sing	we	

Decoding skills taught to date: consonants *m, s, t, c*; short *a*; consonant *n*; consonant *d*; consonant *p*; consonant *f*; short *i*; consonant *r*; consonant *h*; consonant *s* /z/; consonant *b*; hard *g*; short *o*; consonant *l*; consonant *x*; inflection *-s*; short *e*; consonant *y*

Six Yams

DECODABLE WORDS

Target Skill: **consonant *y***

yams	Yan	yes	

Previously Taught Skills

big	fit	in	Mom
can	fix	mix	pan
Dad	hot	mmmm	six

SKILLS APPLIED IN WORDS IN STORY: consonants *m, s, t, c*; short *a*; consonant *n*; consonant *d*; consonant *p*; consonant *f*; short *i*; consonant *h*; consonant *s* /z/; consonant *b*; hard *g*; short *o*; consonant *x*; inflection -*s*; short *e*; consonant *y*

HIGH-FREQUENCY WORDS

a	do	helps	the
and	have	like	they

Houghton Mifflin Harcourt.

Six Yams

Jed can help Dad.
His hens get fed.

Pat can help Mom.
Pat gets Mom all set.

Big Red Rags begs to play.
Meg can help Big Red Rags.

We **can** help!

short *e*

BOOK 32

We Can Help

Ben can help Mom.
Ben gets bags and cans.

High-Frequency Words Taught to Date

Grade 1

a	do	go	I	my	the	what
all	does	have	is	no	they	who
and	find	he	like	play	to	with
are	for	help	look	see	too	you
be	funny	here	me	sing	we	

Decoding skills taught to date: consonants *m, s, t,* c; short *a*; consonant *n*; consonant *d*; consonant *p*; consonant *f*; short *i*; consonant *r*; consonant *h*; consonant *s*/z/; consonant *b*; consonant *g* (hard); short *o*; consonant *l*; consonant *x*; inflection *-s*; short *e*

We Can Help

DECODABLE WORDS

Target Skill: **short *e***

begs	fed	gets	Jed	Red
Ben	get	hens	Meg	set

Previously Taught Skills

bags	can	Dad	Mom	Rags
Big	cans	his	Pat	

SKILLS APPLIED IN WORDS IN STORY: consonants *m, s, t, c*; short *a*; consonant *n*; consonant *d*; consonant *p*; consonant *f*; short *i*; consonant *r*; consonant *h*; consonant *s* /z/; consonant *b*; consonant *g* (hard); short *o;* inflection *–s*; short *e*

HIGH-FREQUENCY WORDS

all	help	to
and	play	we

Houghton Mifflin Harcourt.

short *e*

BOOK 32

We Can Help

Meg met Big Red.
Meg can not pet him.

A hen! A hen!
Meg can not get in the pen.

What did Meg get to do?
Meg fed Ram.

Meg

Here is a fox den.
Let Fox nap in his den, Meg.

High-Frequency Words Taught to Date

Grade 1

a	do	go	I	my	the	with
all	does	have	is	no	they	what
and	find	he	like	play	to	who
are	for	help	look	see	too	you
be	funny	here	me	sing	we	

Decoding skills taught to date: consonants *m, s, t, c*; short *a*; consonant *n*; consonant *d*; consonant *p*; consonant *f*; short *i*; consonant *r*; consonant *h*; consonant *s* /z/; consonant *b*,; consonant *g* (hard); short *o*; consonant *l*; consonant *x*; inflection *-s*; short *e*

Meg

DECODABLE WORDS

Target Skill: **short *e***

den	get	let	met	pet
fed	hen	Meg	pen	Red

Previously Taught Skills

Big	fox	his	nap
can	has	in	not
did	him	is	Ram

SKILLS APPLIED IN WORDS IN STORY: consonants *m, t,* c; short *a*; consonant *n*; consonant *d*; consonant *p*; consonant *f*; short *i*; consonant *r*; consonant *h*; consonant s /z/; consonant *b*; consonant *g* (hard); short *o*; consonant *l*; consonant *x*; short *e*

HIGH-FREQUENCY WORDS

a	here	to
do	the	what

Houghton Mifflin Harcourt

short *e*

BOOK 31

Meg

Dad has big, big logs.
The Labs help Dad.

Dad has bags and cans.
Labs fit the bags and cans in bins!

Dad sits.
The Labs like naps, naps, naps!

Dad Has Labs

Dad has dogs.
The dogs are Labs.
The Labs help Dad.

High-Frequency Words Taught to Date

Grade 1

a	do	go	I	no	the	we
and	find	have	is	play	they	what
are	for	he	like	see	to	with
be	funny	help	look	sing	too	you

Decoding skills taught to date: consonants *m, s, c, t*; short *a*; consonant *n*; consonant *d*; consonant *p*; consonant *f*; short *i*; consonant *r*; consonant *h*; final /z/ spelled *s*; consonant *b*; consonant *g* (hard); short *o*; consonant *l*; consonant *x*; inflection *-s*

Dad Has Labs

DECODABLE WORDS

Target Skill: **inflection *-s***

bags	cans	Labs	naps
bins	dogs	logs	sits

Previously Taught Skills

big	fit	in
Dad	has	

SKILLS APPLIED IN WORDS IN STORY: consonants *s, c, t*; short *a*; consonant *n*; consonant *d*; consonant *p*; consonant *f*; short *i*; consonant *h*; consonant *s* /z/; consonant *b*; consonant *g* (hard); short *o*; consonant *l*; inflection *-s*

HIGH-FREQUENCY WORDS

and	help	the
are	like	

Houghton Mifflin Harcourt

inflection *-s*

BOOK 30

Dad Has Labs

Dads get hot dogs!

Dads get hams!

Deb and Tom get cans.

They sip pop!

The Moms and dads ran.
Deb, Tom, and Pam ran, too!

inflection -*s*

BOOK 29

Moms, Dads, Kids!

See the moms, dads, and kids.

High-Frequency Words Taught to Date

Grade 1

a	do	go	I	no	the	we
and	find	have	is	play	they	what
are	for	he	like	see	to	with
be	funny	help	look	sing	too	you

Decoding skills taught to date: consonants *m, s, c, t*; short *a*; consonant *n*; consonant *d*; consonant *p*; consonant *f*; short *i*; consonant *r*; consonant *h*; final /z/ spelled *s*; consonant *b*; consonant *g* (hard); short *o*; consonant *l*; consonant *x*; inflection *-s*

Moms, Dads, Deb, Tom, and Pam

DECODABLE WORDS

Target Skill: **inflection *-s***

cans	dogs	kids	
dads	hams	moms	

Previously Taught Skills

Deb	hot	pop	sip
get	Pam	ran	Tom

SKILLS APPLIED IN WORDS IN STORY: consonants *m, s, c, t*; short *a*; consonant *n*; consonant *d*; consonant *p*; short *i*; consonant *r*; consonant *h*; consonant *b*; consonant *g* (hard); short *o*; inflection *-s*

HIGH-FREQUENCY WORDS

and	see	the	they	too

Houghton Mifflin Harcourt

inflection *-s*

BOOK 29

Moms, Dads, Deb, Tom, and Pam

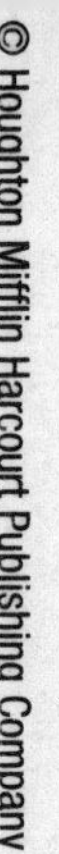

Max is big.
Max is six, six, six!

Max has a big, big box.

A big, big fox!
A big fox for big Max.

Max Is Six

Max is six.
Six, six, six!

High-Frequency Words Taught to Date

Grade 1

a	do	go	I	no	the	we
and	find	have	is	play	they	what
are	for	he	like	see	to	with
be	funny	help	look	sing	too	you

Decoding skills taught to date: consonants *m, s, c, t*; short *a*; consonant *n*; consonant *d*; consonant *p*; consonant *f*; short *i*; consonant *r*; consonant *h*; final /z/ spelled *s*; consonant *b*; consonant *g* (hard); short *o*; consonant *l*; consonant *x*

Max Is Six

DECODABLE WORDS

Target Skill:	**consonant *x***
box	Max
fox	six

Previously Taught Skills

big

has

SKILLS APPLIED IN WORDS IN STORY: consonants *m, s, c, t*; short *a*; consonant *f*; short *i*; consonant *h*; consonant *s* /z/; consonant *b*; consonant *g* (hard); short *o*; consonant *x*

HIGH-FREQUENCY WORDS

a	is
for	

Houghton Mifflin Harcourt.

Max Is Six

Max can mix.

Mix it, Max. Mix it!

Can Max fix it?

Fix it, Max. Fix it!

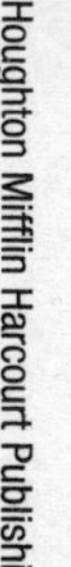

Max Can Mix

Mom has a box.

High-Frequency Words Taught to Date

Grade 1

a	do	go	I	no	the	we
and	find	have	is	play	they	what
are	for	he	like	see	to	with
be	funny	help	look	sing	too	you

Decoding skills taught to date: consonants *m, s, c, t*; short *a*; consonant *n*; consonant *d*; consonant *p*; consonant *f*; short *i*; consonant *r*; consonant *h*; final /z/ spelled *s*; consonant *b*; consonant *g* (hard); short *o*; consonant *l*; consonant *x*

Max Can Mix

DECODABLE WORDS

Target Skill: **consonant *x***

box	Max
fix	mix

Previously Taught Skills:

can	it
has	Mom

SKILLS APPLIED IN WORDS IN STORY: consonants *m, s, c, t*; short *a*; consonant *n*; consonant *f*; short *i*; consonant *h*; final /z/ spelled *s*; consonant *b*; short *o*; consonant *x*

HIGH-FREQUENCY WORDS

a

Houghton Mifflin Harcourt

Max Can Mix

Lon can find Mom.

Mom can see it is bad.

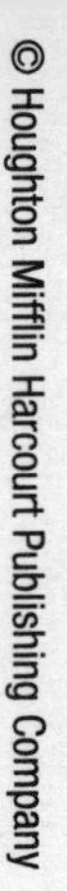

Lon is on a lap.

Mom sat with Lon.

Mom can help him.

"Have a sip, Lon.
It can help."
Lon did sip a lot!

Lon

Lon hit a big, big log.

High-Frequency Words Taught to Date

Grade 1

a	do	go	I	no	the	we
and	find	have	is	play	they	what
are	for	he	like	see	to	with
be	funny	help	look	sing	too	you

Decoding skills taught to date: consonants *m, s, t, c*; short *a*; consonant *n*; consonant *d*; consonant *p*; consonant *f*; short *i*; consonant *r*; consonant *h*; consonant *s* /z/; consonant *b*; consonant *g* (hard); short *o*; consonant *l*

DECODABLE WORDS

Target Skill: **consonant *l***

lap	log	Lon	lot	

Previously Taught Skills

bad	did	is	Mom	sat
big	hit	it	on	sip
can				

SKILLS APPLIED IN WORDS IN STORY: consonants *m, s, t, c*; short *a*; consonant *n*; consonant *d*; consonant *p*; short *i*; consonant *h*; consonant *s* /z/; consonant *b*; consonant *g* (hard); short *o*; consonant *l*

HIGH-FREQUENCY WORDS

a	have	see
find	help	with

Houghton Mifflin Harcourt.

consonant *l*

BOOK 26

Lon

Can a big bat fit?

Lin can fit a big bat in the bin!

Can a lot fit?

Lin can fit a lot in the bin!

Can the lid fit on the big bin?
Lin can fit the lid on the big bin!

A Big Bin

Can a bib fit in the big bin?
Lin can fit the bib in the big bin.

High-Frequency Words Taught to Date

Grade 1

a	do	go	I	no	the	we
and	find	have	is	play	they	what
are	for	he	like	see	to	with
be	funny	help	look	sing	too	you

Decoding skills taught to date: consonants *m, s, t,* c; short *a*; consonant *n*; consonant *d*; consonant *p*; consonant *f*; short *i*; consonant *r*; consonant *h*; consonant *s* /z/; consonant *b*; consonant *g* (hard); short *o*; consonant *l*

A Big Bin

DECODABLE WORDS

Target Skill: **consonant *l***

lid	Lin	lot

Previously Taught Skills

bat	big	can	in
bib	bin	fit	on

SKILLS APPLIED IN WORDS IN STORY: consonants *t, c*; short *a*; consonant *n*; consonant *d*; consonant *f*; short *i*; consonant *b*; consonant *g* (hard); short *o*; consonant *l*

HIGH-FREQUENCY WORDS

a	the

Houghton Mifflin Harcourt

consonant *l*

BOOK 25

A Big Bin

Dot and Dom hop on top.

Hop! Hop! Hop!

Dom and Dot hop on top.

Hop! Hop! Hop!

Dot and Dom do not hop.
They **nap**!

Hop! Hop! Hop!

Dot and Dom can hop.
Hop! Hop! Hop!

High-Frequency Words Taught to Date

Grade 1

a	do	go	I	no	the	we
and	find	have	is	play	they	what
are	for	he	like	see	to	with
be	funny	help	look	sing	too	you

Decoding skills taught to date: consonants *m, s, t, c*; short *a*; consonant *n*; consonant *d*; consonant *p*; consonant *f*; short *i*; consonant *r*; consonant *h*; consonant *s* /z/; consonant *b*; consonant *g* (hard); short *o*

Hop! Hop! Hop!

DECODABLE WORDS

Target Skill: **short *o***

Dom	hop	on
Dot	not	top

Previously Taught Skills

can

nap

SKILLS APPLIED IN WORDS IN STORY: consonants *m, t, c*; short *a*; consonant *n*; consonant *d*; consonant *p*; consonant *h*; short *o*

HIGH-FREQUENCY WORDS

and

do

they

Houghton Mifflin Harcourt

short *o*

BOOK 24

Hop! Hop! Hop!

What can Don Dog do?
Don can hop, hop, hop!

Mom and Dad do not hop.
Mom and Dad are mad.

Don Dog is sad.
He has to mop.
Mop, mop, mop!

Don Dog

What can Don Dog do?
Don can dig a big pit!

High-Frequency Words Taught to Date

Grade 1

a	do	go	I	no	the	we
and	find	have	is	play	they	what
are	for	he	like	see	to	with
be	funny	help	look	sing	too	you

Decoding skills taught to date: consonants *m, s, t, c*; short *a*; consonant *n*; consonant *d*; consonant *p*; consonant *f*; short *i*; consonant *r*; consonant *h*; consonant *s* /z/; consonant *b*; consonant *g* (hard); short *o*

Don Dog

DECODABLE WORDS

Target Skill: **short *o***

dog	hop	mop
Don	Mom	not

Previously Taught Skills

big	dig	mad
can	has	pit
Dad	is	sad

SKILLS APPLIED IN WORDS IN STORY: consonants *m, s, t, c*; short *a*; consonant *n*; consonant *d*; consonant *p*; short *i*; consonant *h*; consonant *s* /z/; consonant *b*; consonant *g* (hard)

HIGH-FREQUENCY WORDS

a	he
and	to
are	what
do	

Houghton Mifflin Harcourt

short *o*

BOOK 23

Don Dog

Pam and the man gab.
"What a big, big fig!"

"Have it, Pam."

Pam had the big, big fig!

Pam bit it.

"Mmm!"

Big, Big Fig

Pam can see a big, big fig.

High-Frequency Words Taught to Date

Grade 1

a	be	have	I	look	the	we	you
and	for	he	is	play	to	what	
are	go	help	like	see	too	with	

Decoding skills taught to date: consonants *m, s, t, c*; short *a*; consonant *n*; consonant *d*; consonant *p*; consonant *f*; short *i*; consonant *r*; consonant *h*; consonant *s* /z/; consonant *b*; consonant *g* (hard)

Big, Big Fig

DECODABLE WORDS

Target Skill: **consonant *g* (hard)**

big gab
fig

Previously Taught Skills

bit	is	Mmm
can	it	Pam
had	man	

SKILLS APPLIED IN WORDS IN STORY: consonants *m, s, t, c*; short *a*; consonant *n*; consonant *d*; consonant *p*; consonant *f*; short *i*; consonant *h*; consonant *s* /z/; consonant *b;* consonant *g* (hard)

HIGH-FREQUENCY WORDS

a	see
and	the
have	what
I	

Houghton Mifflin Harcourt

consonant *g* (hard)

BOOK 22

Big, Big Fig

Tim can tag Mag.

Tag!

Mag can tag Tim, too.

Tag!

Mag and Tim like tag.
Tag is a big hit!

consonant *g* (hard)

Tag!

Mag and Tim can play tag.

High-Frequency Words Taught to Date

Grade 1

a	for	help	look	to	with
and	go	I	play	too	you
are	have	is	see	we	
be	he	like	the	what	

Decoding skills taught to date: consonants *m, s, t, c*; short *a*; consonant *n*; consonant *d*; consonant *p*; consonant *f*; short *i*; consonant *r*; consonant *h*; consonant *s* /z/; consonant *b*; consonant *g* (hard)

Tag!

DECODABLE WORDS

Target Skill: **consonant *g* (hard)**

big	tag
Mag	

Previously Taught Skills

can	is
hit	Tim

SKILLS APPLIED IN WORDS IN STORY: consonants *m, t, c*; short *a*; consonant *n*; short *i*; consonant *b*

HIGH-FREQUENCY WORDS

a	play
and	too
like	

Houghton Mifflin Harcourt

consonant *g* (hard)

BOOK 21

Tag!

Pam had a big hit.
Pam ran and ran.

Nan can bat, too.
Nan can hit a bit.

Nan had a big hit, too!
Nan can go fast.
Dad is a big fan!

Pam and Nan

Pam can bat.
Pam can hit.

High-Frequency Words Taught to Date

Grade 1

a	for	help	look	to	with
and	go	I	play	too	you
are	have	is	see	we	
be	he	like	the	what	

Decoding skills taught to date: consonants *m, s, t, c*; short *a*; consonant *n*; consonant *d*; consonant *p*; consonant *f*; short *i*; consonant *r*; consonant *h*; consonant *s* /z/; consonant *b*

Pam and Nan

DECODABLE WORDS

Target Skill: consonant *b*

bat	big	bit		

Previously Taught Skills

can	fan	had	is	Pam
Dad	fast	hit	Nan	ran

SKILLS APPLIED IN WORDS IN STORY: consonants *m, s, t, c*; short *a*; consonant *n*; consonant *d*; consonant *p*; consonant *f*; short *i*; consonant *r*; consonant *h*; consonant *b*

HIGH-FREQUENCY WORDS

a	and	go	too

Houghton Mifflin Harcourt

consonant *b*

BOOK 20

Pam and Nan

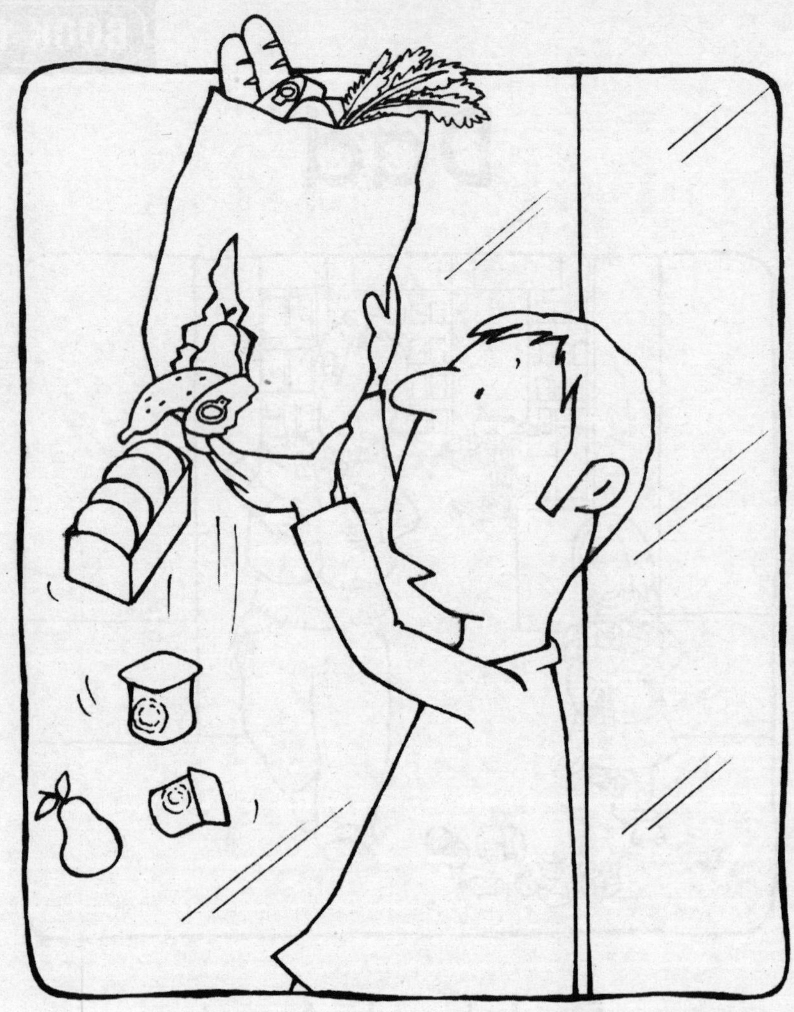

Dad can see it is bad.
Can Dad help?

Can Dad fit it in?
I can help a bit.

Dad did it!

Dad

Dad, look! A rip!

It is bad.

High-Frequency Words Taught to Date

Grade 1

a	for	help	look	to	with
and	go	I	play	too	you
are	have	is	see	we	
be	he	like	the	what	

Decoding skills taught to date: consonants *m, s, t, c*; short *a*; consonant *n*; consonant *d*; consonant *p*; consonant *f*; short *i*; consonant *r*; consonant *h*; consonant *s* /z/; consonant *b*

Dad

DECODABLE WORDS

Target Skill: **consonant *b***

bad bit

Previously Taught Skills

can	did	in	it
Dad	fit	is	rip

SKILLS APPLIED IN WORDS IN STORY: consonants *t*, *c*; short *a*; consonant *n*; consonant *d*; consonant *p*; consonant *f*; short *i*; consonant *r*; consonant *s* /z/; consonant *b*

HIGH-FREQUENCY WORDS

a help I look see

Houghton Mifflin Harcourt

consonant *b*

BOOK 19

Dad

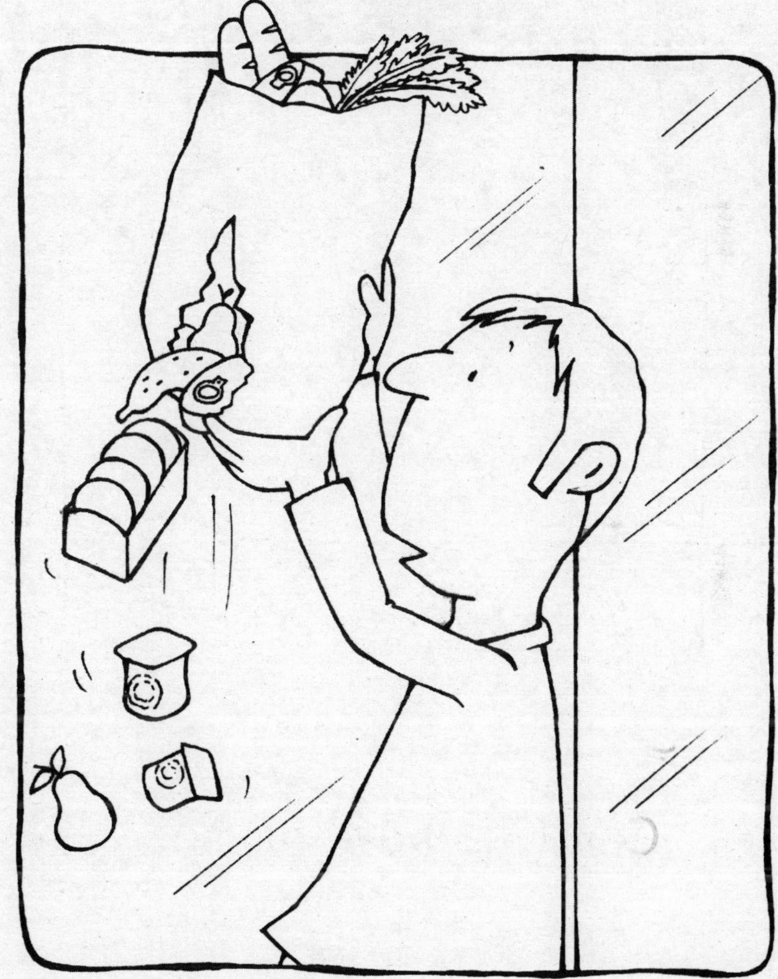

Can Hap have his hat?

Is Hap mad?

Can Hap have his hat?

Can Hap go for his hat?

Hap has his hat!
His hat can fit him.
Hap can play with you!

Hap Has a Hat

Look at Hap.
Hap can see his hat.

High-Frequency Words Taught to Date

a	be	have	I	look	the	we	you
and	for	he	is	play	to	what	
are	go	help	like	see	too	with	

Decoding skills taught to date: consonants *m, s, t, c*; short *a*; consonant *n*; consonant *d*; consonant *p*; consonant *f*; short *i*; consonant *r*; consonant *h*; consonant *s* /z/

Hap Has a Hat

DECODABLE WORDS

Target Skill: **consonant *s* /z/**

has	his	is	

Previously Taught Skills

at	fit	hat	mad
can	Hap	him	

SKILLS APPLIED IN WORDS IN STORY: consonants *m, t, c,* short *a*; consonant *n*; consonant *d*; consonant *p*; consonant *f*; short *i*; consonant *h*; consonant *s* /z/

HIGH-FREQUENCY WORDS

a	go	look	see	you
for	have	play	with	

Houghton Mifflin Harcourt.

consonant *s* /z/

BOOK 18

Hap Has a Hat

Hal can help Dad with Sam.

Hal can play with Sam.

This hat can fit Sam.
Sam is mad.
Dad can help Sam.

Sam

Hal has Sam in his lap.

High-Frequency Words Taught to Date

Grade 1

a	for	help	look	to	with
and	go	I	play	too	you
are	have	is	see	we	
be	he	like	the	what	

Decoding skills taught to date: consonants *m, s, t, c*; short *a*; consonant *n*; consonant *d*; consonant *p*; consonant *f*; short *i*; consonant *r*; consonant *h*; consonant *s* /z/

Sam

DECODABLE WORDS

Target Skill: **consonant *s* /z/**

has	his	is

Previously Taught Skills

Dad	hat	lap
Hal	in	Sam

SKILLS APPLIED IN WORDS IN STORY: consonants *m, s, t, c*; short *a*; consonant *n*; consonant *d*; consonant *p*; consonant *f*; short *i*; consonant *h*; consonant *s* /z/

HIGH-FREQUENCY WORDS

help	play	this	with

Houghton Mifflin Harcourt

Sam

"Did you see Sam?"

"Sam? Sam has a hat."

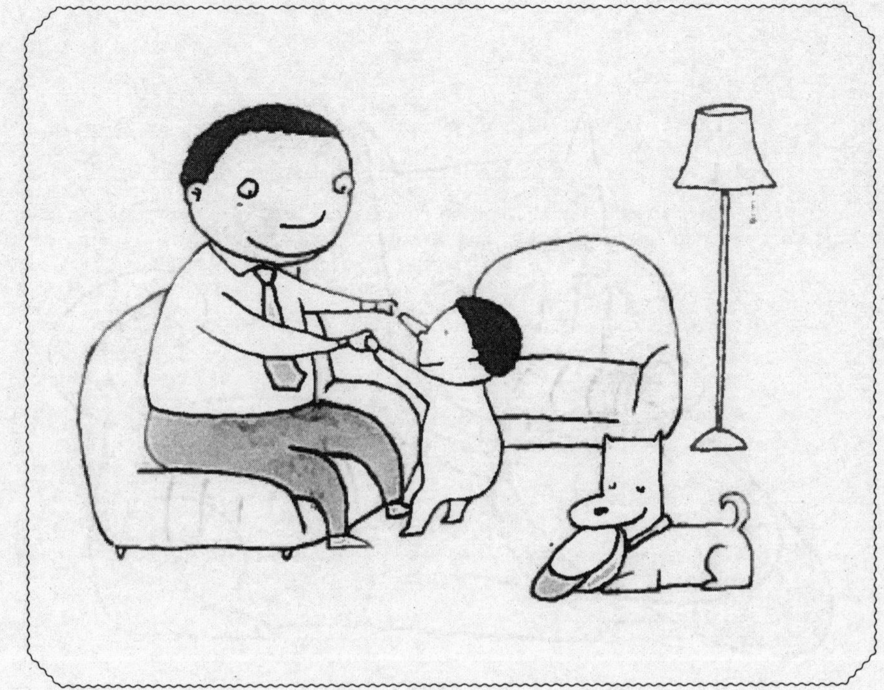

"Dad, look at him.
Sam has it!
Sam has it!"

"Sam had the hat.
Sam did it.
Sam, Sam, Sam!"

Sam Has a Hat

"Did you see a hat?"

"A hat? See if Sam has it."

High-Frequency Words Taught to Date

Grade 1

a	for	help	look	to	with
and	go	I	play	too	you
are	have	is	see	we	
be	he	like	the	what	

Decoding skills taught to date: consonants *m, s, t, c*; short *a*; consonant *n*; consonant *d*; consonant *p*; consonant *f*; short *i*; consonant *r*; consonant *h*

Sam Has a Hat

DECODABLE WORDS

Target Skill: **consonant *h***

had	hid
has	him
hat	

Previously Taught Skills

at	him	Sam
dad	if	
did	it	

SKILLS APPLIED IN WORDS IN STORY: consonants *m, s, t*; short *a*; consonant *d*; consonant *f*; short *i*; consonant *h*

HIGH-FREQUENCY WORDS

a	see	with
look	the	you

Houghton Mifflin Harcourt.

consonant *h*

BOOK 16

Sam Has a Hat

Did Sam have ham?
We had ham for him.

Mim had ham.

Ham! Ham! We had ham!

consonant *h*

We Had Ham

Ham! Ham! We like ham!

High-Frequency Words Taught to Date

Grade 1

a	for	help	look	to	with
and	go	I	play	too	you
are	have	is	see	we	
be	he	like	the	what	

Decoding skills taught to date: consonants *m, s, t, c*; short *a*; consonant *n*; consonant *d*; consonant *p*; consonant *f*; short *i*; consonant *r*; consonant *h*

We Had Ham

DECODABLE WORDS

Target Skill: **consonant *h***

had him
ham

Previously Taught Skills

did
Mim
Sam

SKILLS APPLIED IN WORDS IN STORY: consonants *m, s*; short *a*; consonant *d*; short *i*; consonant *h*

HIGH-FREQUENCY WORDS

for like
have we

Houghton Mifflin Harcourt

consonant *h*

BOOK 15

We Had Ham

I ran, ran, ran.

It is Nan!

Rip, rip, rip.

I like it!

Nan can sit.
I can play!

I Can Play!

Rap, rap, rap!
Is it Nan?

High-Frequency Words Taught to Date

Grade 1

a	for	help	look	to	with
and	go	I	play	too	you
are	have	is	see	we	
be	he	like	the	what	

Decoding skills taught to date: consonants *m, s, t, c*; short *a*; consonant *n*; consonant *d*; consonant *p*; consonant *f*; short *i*; consonant *r*

I Can Play!

DECODABLE WORDS

Target Skill: **consonant *r***

ran rip
rap

Previously Taught Skills

can Nan
is sit
it

SKILLS APPLIED IN WORDS IN STORY: consonants *m, s, c*; short *a*; consonant *n*; consonant *d*; consonant *p*; short *i*; consonant *r*

HIGH-FREQUENCY WORDS

I
like
play

Houghton Mifflin Harcourt.

I Can Play!

Ric can see the rim.

Miss Pam can help Ric.

It can go in.
Miss Pam is a fan!

consonant *r*

BOOK 13

Ric

Ric ran.
Ric ran in.

High-Frequency Words Taught to Date

Grade 1

a	for	help	look	to	with
and	go	I	play	too	you
are	have	is	see	we	
be	he	like	the	what	

Decoding skills taught to date: consonants *m, s, t, c*; short *a*; consonant *n*; consonant *d*; consonant *p*; consonant *f*; short *i*; consonant *r*

Ric

DECODABLE WORDS

Target Skill: **consonant *r***

ran Ric rim

Previously Taught Skills

can	fit	it	Pam
fan	in	Miss	

SKILLS APPLIED IN WORDS IN STORY: consonants *m, s, t, c*; short *a*; consonant *n*; consonant *p*; consonant *f*; short *i*; consonant *r*

HIGH-FREQUENCY WORDS

a	help	see
go	is	the

Houghton Mifflin Harcourt

Ric

Sid did it!
Sid can be fast!

Can Sid sit?

Sid did it!
Sid can sit!

Sid

Can Sid be fast?

High-Frequency Words Taught to Date

Grade 1

a	go	is	the	with
and	have	like	to	you
are	he	look	too	
be	help	play	we	
for	I	see	what	

Decoding skills taught to date: consonants *m, s, t, c*; short *a*; consonant *n*; consonant *d*; consonant *p*; consonant *f*; short *i*

Sid

DECODABLE WORDS

Target Skill: **short *i***

did	Sid
it	sit

Previously Taught Skills

can	fast

SKILLS APPLIED IN WORDS IN STORY: consonants *s, t, c*; short *a*; consonant *n*; consonant *d*; consonant *f*; short *i*

HIGH-FREQUENCY WORDS

be

Houghton Mifflin Harcourt

short *i*

BOOK 12

Sid

Tim is fast, too.
Tim can help Nan.

Did it fit, Nan?
It did! It did!

Nan and Tim can sit and sip.

Nan and Tim

Go fast, Nan.

High-Frequency Words Taught to Date

Grade 1

a	for	help	look	to	with
and	go	I	play	too	you
are	have	is	see	we	
be	he	like	the	what	

Decoding skills taught to date: consonants *m, s, t, c*; short *a*; consonant *n*; consonant *d*; consonant *p*; consonant *f*; short *i*

Nan and Tim

DECODABLE WORDS

Target Skill: **short *i***

did	it	sit
fit	sip	Tim

Previously Taught Skills

can
fast
Nan

SKILLS APPLIED IN WORDS IN STORY: consonants *s, t, c*; short *a*; consonant *n*; consonant *d*; consonant *p*; consonant *f*; short *i*

HIGH-FREQUENCY WORDS

and	help	too
go	is	

Houghton Mifflin Harcourt

short *i*

BOOK 11

Nan and Tim

A fat, fat cat?

Fat cat! Fat cat! Fat cat!
Help, Dad!

We like Nat.

Fat Cat

I am sad, Nat.

High-Frequency Words Taught to Date

Grade 1

a	go	like	to
and	help	play	we
are	I	see	with
be	is	the	you

Decoding skills taught to date: consonants *m, s, t, c*; short *a*; consonant *n*; consonant *d*; consonant *p*; consonant *f*

Fat Cat

DECODABLE WORDS

Target Skill: **consonant *f***

fat

Previously Taught Skills

am	sad
cat	
Nat	

SKILLS APPLIED IN WORDS IN STORY: consonants *m, s, t, c*; short *a*; consonant *n*; consonant *d*; consonant *f*

HIGH-FREQUENCY WORDS

a	like
help	we
I	

Houghton Mifflin Harcourt.

consonant *f*

BOOK 10

Fat Cat

Fan the cat, Sam.

Fan Pam, Sam.

The cat can fan Sam.
Pam can fan Sam.
Fan, fan, fan.

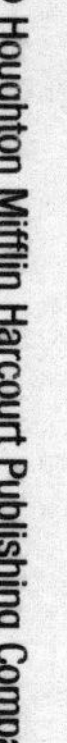

Fan, Fan, Fan

Fat Sam can fan.
Fan, fan, fan.

High-Frequency Words Taught to Date

Grade 1

a	go	like	to
and	help	play	we
are	I	see	with
be	is	the	you

Decoding skills taught to date: consonants *m, s, t, c*; short *a*; consonant *n*; consonant *d*; consonant *p*; consonant *f*

Fan, Fan, Fan

DECODABLE WORDS

Target Skill: **consonant *f***

fan fat

Previously Taught Skills

can cat Pam Sam

SKILLS APPLIED IN WORDS IN STORY: consonants *m, s, t, c*; short *a*; consonant *n*; consonant *p*; consonant *f*

HIGH-FREQUENCY WORDS

the

Houghton Mifflin Harcourt.

consonant *f*

BOOK 9

Fan, Fan, Fan

Pam can tap.

Pat can tap.

Go, Pam.

Go, Pat.

Tap! Tap! Tap!

Tap, Tap, Tap

Pam and Pat tap.

High-Frequency Words Taught to Date

a	go	like	to
and	help	play	we
are	I	see	with
be	is	the	you

Decoding skills taught to date: consonants: *m, s, t, c*; short *a*; consonant *n*; consonant *d*; consonant *p*

Tap, Tap, Tap

DECODABLE WORDS

Target Skill: **Consonant *p***

Pam Pat tap

Previously Taught Skills

can

SKILLS APPLIED IN WORDS IN STORY: consonants *m, t, c*; short *a*; consonant *n*; consonant *p*

HIGH-FREQUENCY WORDS

and go

Houghton Mifflin Harcourt.

Tap, Tap, Tap

Tap, tap, tap.
I can tap.

Tap, tap, tap.
Can Pat nap?

Sap! Pat is sad.
Can you help Pat?

Can Pat Nap?

Pat can nap.

High-Frequency Words Taught to Date

Grade 1

a	go	like	to
and	help	play	we
are	I	see	with
be	is	the	you

Decoding skills taught to date: consonants: *m, s, t, c*; short *a*; consonant *n*; consonant *d*; consonant *p*

Can Pat Nap?

DECODABLE WORDS

Target Skill: **consonant *p***

nap Pat sap tap

Previously Taught Skills

can sad

SKILLS APPLIED IN WORDS IN STORY: consonants *s, t, c,* short *a*; consonant *n*; consonant *d*; consonant *p*

HIGH-FREQUENCY WORDS

help I is you

Houghton Mifflin Harcourt

consonant *p*

BOOK 7

Can Pat Nap?

Tad! Tad! Tad!

Dan is mad.
Mad, mad, mad.

Is Dan mad?
Dan and Tad play.

Tad

Tad can play.

High-Frequency Words Taught to Date

Grade 1

a	go	like	to
and	help	play	we
are	I	see	with
be	is	the	you

Decoding skills taught to date: consonants: *m, s, t, c*; short *a*; consonant *n*; consonant *d*

Tad

DECODABLE WORDS

Target Skill: **consonant *d***

Dan mad Tad

Previously Taught Skills

can

SKILLS APPLIED IN WORDS IN STORY: consonants: *m, s, t, c*; short *a*; consonant *n*; consonant *d*

HIGH-FREQUENCY WORDS

and is play

Houghton Mifflin Harcourt

consonant *d*

BOOK 6

Tad